Duration introduction

• • long • • short • • rhythm • • pulse • • beat • • metre • • silence • •

 KU-361-861

ABOUT THE STARTER ACTIVITY

Four beat body beat WB — combining pulse and rhythm in a simple percussion game.

WHAT YOU NEED TO KNOW ABOUT DURATION

★ Music is made up of sounds and silences of different duration.

★ Groupings of sounds and silences make rhythms.

★ Pulse or beat is like the steady tap of walking feet. When it is not audible, it is like a silently swinging pendulum behind the music.

★ The beat of music can be organised into metre, a regular grouping of accented beats with the strongest emphasis on beat 1, eg

2 metre (accent on 1)   I 2 I 2 I 2 I 2

3 metre (accent on 1)   I 2 3 I 2 3 I 2 3 I 2 3

4 metre (accent on 1 and 3)   I 2 3 4 I 2 3 4 I 2 3 4

★ When a beat, which is usually weak, is instead accented, the effect is called syncopation:

4 metre (accent on 2 and 4)   I 2 3 4 I 2 3 4 I 2 3 4

★ A pattern of sounds which is repeated throughout a piece of music is called an ostinato.

What you will need

• Printouts of the number cards and rhythms. WB

• A small selection of percussion instruments.

Teaching tip

Change the numbers of the groups and invite volunteers to conduct with the cards. If a group's card is shown a second time, it drops out until shown the card again.

You can hear a sample of the game on CD track 1; the instruments enter in group order: 1 3 4 2.

Four beat body beat

1. Talk about body percussion, and ask the children to demonstrate some ideas, eg:

2. Select four suggestions and divide the class into four corresponding groups, eg stampers, clappers, knee tappers, finger clickers. Give each group a number from one to four and show them the four number cards.

3. All count 'one, two, three, four' to a steady beat (ask one child to play the pulse on a drum to support this). Hold up one of the number cards – the corresponding group makes their sound on the corresponding count, eg

   I   **2**   3   4   I   **2**   3   4

4. While the first group continues, hold up another card to add another group's sound, until all four groups are playing:

   I   **2**   **3**   **4**   I   **2**   3   **4**

5. Now select one confident individual from each group and give each their group's rhythm card printout and a percussion instrument, eg wood block, tambour, finger cymbals, maracas. Each child plays their rhythm starting on their group's number, when their group's number is shown, eg group 2:

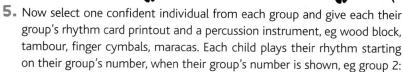

   I   **2**   3   4   I   **2**   3   4

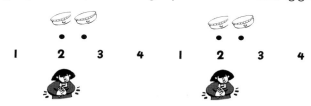

Duration Unsquare dance

• • long • • • short • • • rhythm • • • pulse • • • beat • • • metre • • • silence • • •

WHAT YOU NEED TO KNOW ABOUT UNSQUARE DANCE

★ Composer: Dave Brubeck (born USA, 1920).

★ Dave Brubeck and his jazz quartet were very popular in the fifties and sixties when Brubeck experimented with combining ideas from western classical music with the complex rhythms of African folk music and the freedom of jazz improvisation.

★ Like many of his pieces, *Unsquare dance* has an odd-number metre – the pulse is grouped in sevens. Eight beats in the metre would have given a more regular feel to the music but, in Brubeck's words, the music 'refuses to be squared'.

★ Brubeck plays the piano solo and the percussionist plays fast, syncopated rhythms, tapping his sticks on the side of the bass drum. Two musicians clap a syncopated ostinato which interlinks with the double bass ostinato and continues throughout the piece.

★ In the *Unsquare dance* activities, the children will be finding out how the composer has used syncopation within a metre of seven beats to make an exciting piece of music, which they can perform.

ABOUT THE ACTIVITIES

Odds and evens – exploring the effect of counting in different metres.

Listen to *Unsquare dance* – counting the metre and noticing the ostinatos.

Unsquare ostinatos `WB` – learning the rhythm of the bass and clapping ostinatos used in *Unsquare dance*.

Combining the ostinatos `WB` – performing the bass and clapping ostinatos together.

Listen to *Unsquare dance* – noticing the combined ostinatos and the tune of the bass ostinato.

Unsquare bass tune – playing the notes of the bass ostinato on tuned percussion.

Listen to *Unsquare dance* – focusing on the improvisations which are added to the ostinatos.

Sevens improvisation – performing the *Unsquare dance* ostinatos and taking turns to add improvisations.

Odds and evens

I. Start the activity by getting everyone to count '1 2 1 2 1 2 ...', while you tap the drum to help keep the beat steady.

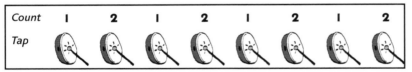

2. Count and tap again, this time clapping on all the number ones – the strong beat of each group:

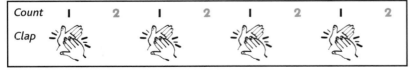

3. Repeat with groupings of three, then four beats, and so on up to nine. Try this at a variety of speeds but remember to keep each tempo steady. Take time to enjoy the feel of each different metre.

4. Repeat the activity from the beginning, choosing an extra number to clap on with each grouping, eg

What you will need

• A drum or a wood block.

Teaching tip
Bring the children in together by first counting one cycle of the number group at the speed you want the children to perform, eg

I 2 3 4 I 2 3 4
Intro

Music Express Extra

102 102 528 3

EFFIELD HALLAM UNIVERSITY
LEARNING CENTRE
WITHDRAWN FROM STOCK

Listening to Music Elements

age 7+

Active listening materials to support a primary music scheme

This book is due for return on or before the last date shown below.

This book is accompanied
by.....2...CD/DVD-ROM(s)

A & C Black • London

Contents

Audio CD – Track list on inside back cover
- All the recordings you need for each activity.

CD-ROM – Photocopiable printouts
- 47 photocopiable printouts for use with the book activities.

CD-ROM – Sample lesson plans
- 7 sample lesson plans showing you how to build the activities into your music scheme of work.
- A handy cross reference to the units of the QCA music scheme of work.

CD-ROM – Interactive whiteboard activities
- 15 interactive whiteboard activities
- Notes to help you get maximum benefit from the interactive activities.

Listen to Unsquare dance

What you will need

The children count quietly in sevens as they listen to track 3 (reference track 2 shows you how to do this). The music is quite fast so the children may need to listen more than once.

Listen again, noticing the clapping pattern this time. There are several claps in each sequence of seven counts. Can the children identify which numbers are clapped? (2, 4, 6, 7.)

Listen again, asking the children to notice what else they can hear in the music. (A double bass plays a repeating pattern which fits together with the clapping pattern. The player plucks the strings with the fingers of the right hand. This playing technique is called pizzicato – pit-zih-kah-to.)

Can the children say on which numbers the double bass plays? (1, 3 and 5.)

Unsquare ostinatos

What you will need

• Printouts of bass ostinato card 1 and clapping ostinato card 2. WB

• A drum or wood block. WB

1. Show the class card 1:

To perform the ostinato, explain that the children will count in sevens and stamp one heel on beats 1, 3 and 5.

2. Divide the class into two groups:

Group 1 – performs the count;

Group 2 – performs the ostinato, tapping heels on 1, 3 and 5.

Swap the groups over so that each has a turn to tap the ostinato.

3. Show card 2:

To perform this ostinato, explain that the children will clap on numbers 2, 4, 6 and 7 – the beats between the bass ostinato.

4. Divide into two groups as in the previous activity.

Group 1 – performs the count;

Group 2 – performs the ostinato, clapping on 2, 4, 6 and 7.

Swap the groups over so that each has a turn to tap the ostinato.

Teaching tip

Track 4 demonstrates the bass ostinato, the clapping ostinato and the ostinatos combined (next page) .

Set a slow count to begin with and count one group of seven to bring everyone in together. When this is confident, try at a faster tempo.

Alternately support the ostinato group by tapping with them and the counting group by counting and tapping the drum to keep the pulse steady.

Duration Unsquare dance

• • long • • short • • rhythm • • pulse • • beat • • metre • • silence • •

Unsquare ostinatos combined

1. Show card 3 – the bass and clapping ostinatos combined:

2. Divide as before into two groups:

   Group 1 – counts and taps heels on 1, 3 and 5;

   Group 2 – counts and claps on 2, 4, 6 and 7.

3. When the children are confident with this, encourage them to count silently and memorise the ostinatos.

4. Now every child taps and claps both ostinatos at the same time.

What you will need

• Printout of combined ostinatos card 3. [WB]

• A drum or wood block. [WB]

Teaching tip
Track 4 demonstrates.

Listen to Unsquare dance

Focus on listening to the combined ostinatos the children have learned to play. Count, tap and clap along with the music.

Questions you might ask

• What is the difference between our bass ostinato and the one we hear played by the double bass? (We are tapping our heels, the double bass plays different notes – a melody.)

On a second listening, you might encourage the children to sing the bass ostinato while quietly clapping the other ostinato.

What you will need

3))

Unsquare bass tune

1. Show the printout grid to the children.

A		G		A		
A		G		A		
D		C		D		
A		G		A		
E		D		E		
A		G		A		

Sing the letter names of the notes as you point to them on the grid.

2. In small groups, the children practise playing the ostinato on the tuned instruments. When this is secure, ask each group to play the bass ostinato while the rest of the children in the class add the clapping ostinato (card 2).

What you will need

5))

• Printout of the bass grid.

• Bass xylophones, keyboards or chime bars with these notes:

G A   C D E

Teaching tip
Track 5 demonstrates the bass ostinato being sung and played.

Listen to Unsquare dance

Revise counting, tapping and playing along with the ostinatos. Now, ask the children to notice what else they hear in the piece.

What you will need

 3))

Questions you might ask

- What other instruments are played and in what order? (Piano, drum sticks on the metal rim of the drum, then piano again.)

- What do you notice about the piano when it plays? (It repeats each of its rhythms several times using different notes.)

- What do the sticks play? (Fast tapping rhythms over the ostinatos.)

Sevens improvisation

What you will need

 6))   6

- Tuned instruments as above.

- Wood blocks, each with pairs of sticks.

- Printout of bass ostinato grid.

Teaching tip

Track 6 demonstrates a Sevens improvisation.

Some children will be able to create new bass ostinatos, using the notes of the original, eg

A E A
G D G...

I. Divide into several small groups. Each group sits in a circle with a set of instruments, and allocates the following roles:

Leader gives a count of seven to start the playing;

1–2 children perform the bass ostinato throughout;

All other children clap the syncopated ostinato;

Individuals take turns to improvise rhythms on the wood block.

2. The group performs their improvisation in this order:

– the leader counts seven to start the playing;

– the bass and clapping ostinatos are played once through;

– as the ostinatos are played again, the first child with the sticks improvises rhythms on the wood block;

– as the ostinatos are played again, the sticks and wood block are passed to the next child to improvise during the next cycle.

Continue until everyone in the clapping group has had a turn.

Duration Inspector Morse

• • long • • short • • rhythm • • pulse • • beat • • metre • • silence • •

WHAT YOU NEED TO KNOW ABOUT INSPECTOR MORSE

★ Composer: Barrington Pheloung (born Sydney, 1954).

★ He wrote the title music of the television crime series, *Inspector Morse*, in 1991.

★ The music begins and ends with an electronic beep which sounds like the dashes and dots of morse code. The rhythm is taken up by the violins which continue repeating it throughout the piece.

ABOUT THE ACTIVITIES

Listen to *Inspector Morse* – recognising the morse signal in the music.

Di daa di daa – communicating simple messages using short and long vocal sounds. The children send and receive signals, encoding and decoding using morse notation.

Secret agents – learning a song, each line of which ends with finger clicks. Later in the activity, the children replace the clicks with simple morse code patterns.

Listen to *Inspector Morse* – decoding the morse signal in the music.

Listen to Inspector Morse

Questions you might ask

• What do you hear at the very beginning of the piece? (An electronic signal, morse code.)

• Do you hear this rhythm again? (Yes, it is played all the way through. The electronic beep comes back at the end.)

• Which instruments play this rhythm? (String instruments, eg violins.)

• Does it change at all? (The rhythm stays the same but it is played as a melody.)

What you will need

🎵 7))

• • long • • short • • rhythm • • pulse • • beat • • metre • • silence • •

What you will need

• Printout of the morse code alphabet.

a • ▬
b ▬ • • •
c ▬ • ▬ •
d ▬ • •
e •
f • • ▬ •
g ▬ ▬ •
h • • • •
i • •
j • ▬ ▬ ▬
k ▬ • ▬
l • ▬ • •
m ▬ ▬
n ▬ •
o ▬ ▬ ▬
p • ▬ ▬ •
q ▬ ▬ • ▬
r • ▬ •
s • • •
t ▬
u • • ▬
v • • • ▬
x ▬ • • ▬
y ▬ • ▬ ▬
z ▬ ▬ • •

Di daa di daa

1. Explain to the children that morse code is a language made up of only two sounds:

   •   short beep (di)

   ▬   long beep (daa)

   Each letter of the alphabet has a corresponding code of up to four units, so that whole words and sentences can be formed from just two basic sounds. To distinguish between the letters and words there is always a short silence between each letter and a longer silence between each word.

2. Show the children the printout of the morse code alphabet. Read through some of the letters with them using di and daa sounds.

3. Listen to track 8, which demonstrates a selection of letters. There is a gap in which the children can copy each signal.

4. Tell the children you are going to spell a word in morse. They will write down each pattern of dots and dashes and then decode it using the morse code printout. Remember to leave a short silence between each letter.

Say	di di di di	di	di daa di di	di daa di di	daa daa daa
Write	• • • •	•	• ▬ • •	• ▬ • •	▬ ▬ ▬
Decode	h	e	l	l	o

Spell out some more words in morse for the children to decode.

Say	daa daa	di di daa	di di di	di di	daa di daa di
Write	▬ ▬	• • ▬	• • •	• •	▬ • ▬ •
Decode	m	u	s	i	c

Say	daa daa	daa daa daa	di daa di	di
Write	▬ ▬	▬ ▬ ▬	• ▬ •	•
Decode	m	o	r	e

5. When the children are familiar with the idea, ask them to work in pairs taking it in turns to relay a simple message in morse vocally to their partner, who writes it down and decodes it.

Secret agents

1. Teach the children this song:

> **Communication, X X X** *(finger clicks)*
> **It's the name of the game, X X X**
> **Signalling morse code across the world, X X X**
> **Electronic bleepers spelling every word. X**

2. When the children are familiar with the song, explain that in place of the finger clicks at the end of each line, they will say a morse letter, which together make up a word ('code'):

> **Communication, daa di daa di,**
> **It's the name of the game, daa daa daa,**
> **Signalling morse code across the world, daa di di,**
> **Electronic bleepers spelling every word, daa.**

Sing the song together, and as a class, decode the word.

Divide the class into two groups:

Secret agent group 1 performs the song and a new morse word card;

Secret agent group 2 listens and decodes the word.

Practise saying the morse letters with group 1 before adding them to the song.

3. When they are ready, the group 1 secret agents sing the song, while the agents in group 2 write down the dot and dash signals. They then decode the new word.

4. Play the game again. This time, divide the class into smaller groups, which each devise their own code cards (extras are provided on printout 8) and practise singing them. The groups perform in turn while the other groups listen and notate the code words. The winning group is the one which cracks most code words.

What you will need

🔘 9)))   🔘 8

• Printouts of the morse 'code' card and extra words.

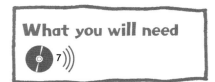

Teaching tip

Teach the song using track 9 (copy song followed by song with code).

The melody is written at the back of the book in staff notation for music readers.

There are extra word cards on printout 8.

Listen to Inspector Morse

Ask the children to focus on the morse signal. Can they write down the pattern of dots and dashes which is repeated throughout, and decode the word? This is not easy. The answer is:

▬ ▬	▬ ▬ ▬	• ▬ •	• • •	•
daa daa	daa daa daa	di daa di	di di di	di
M	**O**	**R**	**S**	**E**

What you will need

🔘 7)))

Duration round up

• • long • • short • • rhythm • • pulse • • beat • • metre • • silence • •

When the children have completed the duration activities in this section, give them opportunities to listen out for and comment on duration in other sections. Here are some examples:

What you will need
🔘 28)))

Tomorrow the fox

Exploring metre: ask the children to tap fingers on palms to mark the pulse of the music as they listen to it. Can they discover how the pulse is grouped in this piece? (It is grouped in twos.)

Can the children suggest some different ways to move which will clearly identify the metre, eg

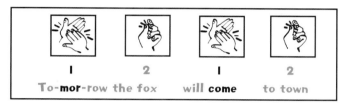

1	**2**	**1**	**2**
To-**mor**-row the fox	will **come**	to town	

What you will need
🔘 39)))

Didlan

Exploring metre: ask the children to tap fingers on palms to mark the pulse of the music as they listen to it. Can they discover how the pulse is grouped in this piece? (It is grouped in threes.)

Can the children suggest some different ways to move which will clearly identify the metre, eg

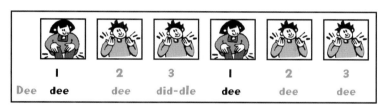

1	**2**	**3**	**1**	**2**	**3**
Dee **dee**	dee	did-dle	**dee**	dee	dee

What you will need
🔘 17)))

La Volta

Exploring ostinato: this version of *La Volta* starts with a pattern of three different low notes repeated again and again on the harpsichord in a three-beat metre. The pattern is an ostinato – it continues throughout while the the melody weaves between the recorder and the higher notes of the harpsichord.

Choose one child to play the ostinato on a tuned instrument.

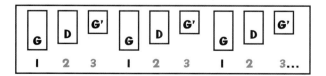

G	D	G'	G	D	G'	G	D	G'
1	**2**	**3**	**1**	**2**	**3**	**1**	**2**	**3...**

Listen to *La Volta*. Can the children recognise the pattern as the same one played on the tuned instrument?

Duration round up

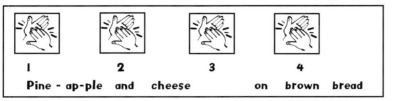

Kartal

Exploring syncopation: this piece is made up of syncopated rhythm patterns within a regular, four-beat metre. The first pattern is repeated many times during the piece, interspersed by other patterns.

As they listen to **Kartal**, ask the children to mark the pulse by tapping their fingers in their palms. The first pattern the kartal plays sounds like, 'pineapple and cheese on brown bread'. Listen carefully; it is quite fast.

1	2	3	4
Pine - ap-ple and	cheese	on	brown bread

> ### Questions you might ask
>
> • What did you notice as you tapped and listened? (Sometimes it was difficult to keep tapping the pulse. The rhythms we heard were different from our tapping. Some of the rhythms did not seem to fit easily with our tapping.)

Divide the class into two groups:

Group 1 – taps the pulse;
Group 2 – says and taps the word rhythm.

Pine - ap-ple and	cheese	on	brown bread
1	2	3	4

When Group 2 can say and tap the rhythm, ask them just to tap the rhythm, saying the words inside their heads. Swap groups.

What you will need

 45))）

Teaching tip

Group the children in pairs to perform the pulse and rhythm together. Encourage them to devise their own syncopated patterns to clap, while their partners keep a steady pulse. Share ideas with the rest of the class.

Transfer the game to pairs of percussion instruments, eg finger cymbals and claves.

ASSESSMENT GUIDANCE

Can the children:

★ perform repeating rhythm patterns on body percussion and untuned percussion?

★ combine repeating rhythms, maintaining their part?

★ improvise rhythms, with awareness of a steady beat?

★ use notations to perform patterns of long and short sounds?

★ understand about metre?

★ use musical vocabulary to describe aspects of beat and rhythm?

Dynamics introduction

• • • loud • • • • quiet • • • • getting louder • • • • getting quieter • • •

ABOUT THE STARTER ACTIVITY

Dynamic shapes [WB] – a game, in which the children recognise and respond in movement to aural signals of loud, medium and quiet.

WHAT YOU NEED TO KNOW ABOUT DYNAMICS

★ Dynamics in music means volume – degrees of loud and quiet.

★ When they write out their music, composers often include dynamic markings, such as **p** for quiet or **f** for loud, to indicate to the performers how the volume should change.

★ In many cultures, music is taught by ear and not from written notation. Dynamics are used, but instead of written markings, an aural signal, such as a rhythm played on a drum, may direct the players to change volume.

What you will need

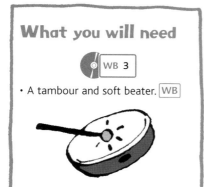

[WB 3]

• A tambour and soft beater. [WB]

• Space in which the children can move freely.

Dynamic shapes

1. Ask the children to move into a clear space.

2. Explain that there are three signals for this game:

 loud tap on the drum – make a star;

 medium tap – feet apart, hands by sides;

 quiet tap – feet together, hands by sides.

3. Try out the signals and check that everyone understands and is able to respond quickly.

4. Now tap the drum three times in this sequence – loud, medium, quiet:

Ask the children what they think this might be telling them to do. Ask a volunteer to demonstrate:

5. Make up different sequences of loud, medium and quiet taps and ask the children to move quietly and quickly into the shapes which indicate the patterns.

6. Give the children turns at signalling – they will quickly discover the need for a clear contrast between the three dynamics.

Dynamics Baris gede 'bandrangan'

• • • loud • • • • quiet • • • • getting louder • • • • getting quieter • •

WHAT YOU NEED TO KNOW ABOUT BARIS GEDE 'BANDRANGAN'

★ Composer: I Wayan Beratha (Indonesia).

★ Beratha is a central figure in Balinese music, working as player and composer, and also as a tuner and gamelan merchant.

★ *Baris gede 'bandrangan'* is a modern piece of gamelan music, composed in 1990, but based on a traditional form.

★ Gamelan is the name of the group of instruments (mainly tuned percussion) as well as the music itself.

★ Gamelan music is an important part of Indonesian life, used for entertainment, at social events and in religious celebration. The traditions of playing go back many centuries and every year competitions are held in Bali to determine the best regional gamelan.

★ Most gamelan have about twenty players, but some are much larger.

★ A baris gede is a ritual spear dance for men; this one is called 'bandrangan' after the tassel attached to the spear's handle.

★ A baris traditionally has a cycle of 2 x 8 beats repeated throughout.

★ Many types of gamelan music include strong contrasts of dynamics. The players learn their parts by ear and, in this example, they follow signals given by the drummer to change to a different volume. In this piece, there are several very quiet sections alternating with very loud sections, and sections in which the volume increases.

★ The instruments heard in Baris gede 'bandrangan' are:

metal gongs of various sizes

metal bars on a frame also various sizes

hand-held cymbal and

drum played with a stick

ABOUT THE ACTIVITIES

Listen to *Baris gede 'bandrangan'* – focusing on the strong contrasts in the dynamics.

Dynamic drummer – expressing loud medium and quiet dynamics in movement, directed by a drum.

Dynamic drum WB – performing a piece of music with contrasting dynamics in the style of a baris. A solo drummer 'conducts' the piece by using a drum to signal changes in dynamics to the players.

Listen to *Baris gede 'bandrangan'* – relating the changes in dynamic to the drum signals in the piece and to the signals in *Dynamic drum*.

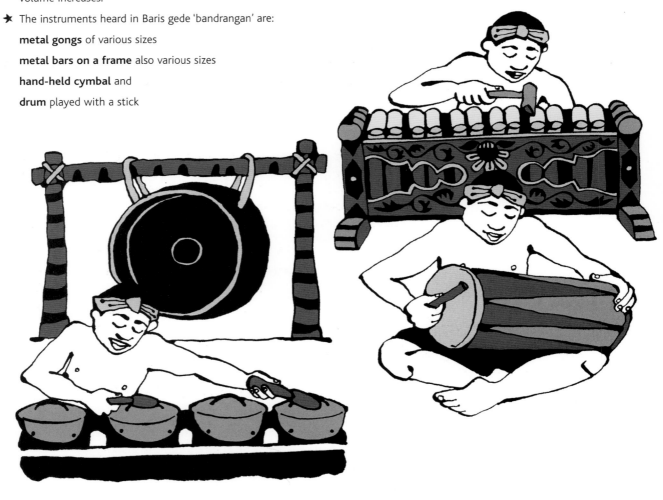

• • • loud • • • • quiet • • • • getting louder • • • • getting quieter • •

What you will need

Listen to Baris gede 'bandrangan'

Focus the children's attention on the strong contrasts and changes of dynamic in the music as they listen. Afterwards discuss the effects.

Questions you might ask

• In the first extract, the instruments repeat their parts many times. How does the volume change? (Sometimes they play loudly, sometimes quietly.)

• Can you describe the dynamics in the second extract after the very fast percussion section? (The instruments play quietly at first, then they grow suddenly louder – crescendo.)

• What happens to the music at the very end of the piece? (It is played gradually more quietly – diminuendo – and slowly.)

Teaching tip

Gamelan pieces are traditionally very long – this piece lasts fifteen minutes. Track 10 is two extracts from the beginning and end of the piece, in which the composer's use of dynamics can be clearly heard.

What you will need

• Space to move freely.

• A drum or tambour and a soft beater.

Dynamic drummer

1. Teach the children this chant. First establish a drum beat to a count of eight, then add the chant to the drum beat:

Count	1	2	3	4	5	6	7	8	1	2	3	4	5	6	7	8
Tap	•	•	•	•	•	•	•	•	•	•	•	•	•	•	•	•
Say	Ba - ris ge- de band-ran-gan, this ba-ris band-ran-gan															

2. Choose one child to be the 'Dynamic drummer'. This child leads the dynamics of the chant by playing the last three beats of the count, loudly or quietly. The rest of the children respond with the loud or quiet body shape from the *Dynamic shapes* activity, and by saying the chant at the appropriate dynamic, eg

Teaching tip

When the children are confident with the loud and quiet signals, try crescendo and diminuendo signals: the chanting children respond with the movements and by making the chant get louder or quieter throughout accordingly.

crescendo • ● ●

diminuendo ● ● •

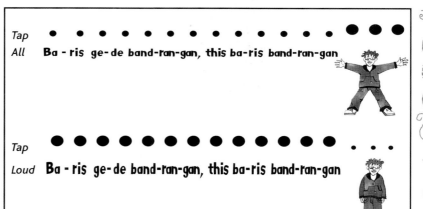

Dynamics Baris gede 'bandrangan'

Dynamic drum

1. Remind the children of the chant from the previous activity and divide the class into three groups. Choose a dynamic drummer again, and teach each group the following movements:

   Group 1 taps shoulders on every syllable of the chant;

   Group 2 claps on every other syllable of the chant;

   Group 3 stamps once on every fourth syllable of the chant:

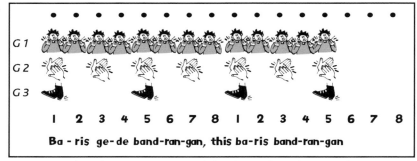

   Ba - ris ge-de band-ran-gan, this ba-ris band-ran-gan

   Notice that the actions stop and the drum plays alone on the last three beats. When the groups can place the actions confidently as they say the chant together, ask the dynamic drummer to lead the dynamics as in the previous activity, each group responding with dynamic shapes during the three solo drum beats followed by the chant at the appropriate dynamic.

2. Repeat the activity, giving each group a set of hand-held percussion, eg finger cymbals for group 1, cymbals for group 2, and cow bells for group 3. The groups substitute instrumental sounds for the actions, and respond to the drum by playing quieter or louder dynamics.

3. Give the same three groups high-, medium- and low- tuned percussion instruments and a printout of the corresponding part.

4. The groups each practise playing their sequences of notes. As before, they use the syllables of the chant to help them identify when to play:

   Group 1 (high) plays a note on every syllable;
   Group 2 (medium) plays a note every second syllable;
   Group 3 (low) plays a note every fourth syllable.

5. When the children are confident at playing their individual parts, try combining them – two at a time first, then all three.

   As before, one child is the dynamic drummer and taps a steady pulse on the drum. To start the piece, the drummer plays one cycle of eight beats to set the opening dynamic and speed.

6. When the combination of parts is secure, ask the drummer to control the dynamics of the piece, directing the groups by playing quiet, medium or loud drum beats during the last three beats of the cycle.

   As the class becomes more confident, the signals can become more demanding, eg

   crescendo   diminuendo

   The drummer may direct the volume to stay the same for any number of repeats, change suddenly, or gradually get louder or quieter.

What you will need

- One large tambour or drum.
- Printout of the dynamic drum chart. WB
- High-, medium- and low-sounding metal untuned percussion, eg finger cymbals, cymbals, cow bells.
- A selection of high-, medium- and low-sounding metal tuned percussion with these notes:

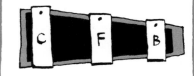

Teaching tip

The piece may be performed by small groups or as a whole class. The tuned percussion specified is the ideal and you may not have enough for the whole class or even for small groups. If necessary, use whatever you do have available with these notes, eg xylophone, piano or keyboard, and supplement with the untuned percussion from the preparatory work.

You can hear a performance of *Dynamic drum* on track 11, in which the parts are introduced one by one along with the chant.

• • • loud • • • • quiet • • • • getting louder • • • • getting quieter • •

Count	1	2	3	4	5	6	7	8	1	2	3	4	5	6	7	8
high	C	C	E	E	F	G	B	B	B	G	F	E	C			
medium	C		E		F		B		B		F		C			
low	C				F				B				C			
	Ba-ris	ge-de			band-ran-gan,this				ba-ris	band-ran	-gan					
drum																
Count	1	2	3	4	5	6	7	8	1	2	3	4	5	6	7	8

What you will need

 10)))

• Space to move freely.

Listen to Baris gede 'bandrangan'

Remind the children of the dynamic body shapes they used to respond to changes in dynamic, eg

crescendo (get louder)

As the music plays, the children respond to the changes in dynamic by adopting the dynamic body shapes.

Teaching tip

The children will naturally respond to the changes in tempo as well as dynamics. Encourage them to respond to the changes in the music by combining the large and small body shapes with slower and faster movements of body parts either on the spot, or travelling if you have a sufficiently large space.

Questions you might ask

• What shape did we make when the drum played loudly/quietly?

• What happens to the music when the drum plays loudly/quietly? (It becomes loud/quiet too.)

• How is this similar to the *Dynamic drum* music we made? (We signalled the music to change by tapping the drum loudly/quietly.)

• How is the music different in the second section? (It is played much faster at first then gradually slows down and gets quieter at the end.)

Dynamics round up

• • • loud • • • • • quiet • • • • getting louder • • • • getting quieter • •

When the children have completed the dynamics activities in this section, give them opportunities to listen out for and comment on dynamics in other sections. Here are some examples:

Five pieces for orchestra, no 1

The composer uses only two dynamics throughout:

pp pianissimo (very quiet);   **ppp** – as quiet as possible.

Each of the instruments plays single notes or very short melodies at the quietest dynamic they can produce.

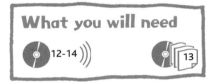

What you will need

🔘 29)))

Questions you might ask

• How would you describe the dynamics? (Very quiet.)

• Do any of the instruments play very loudly? (No.)

• What is the effect of the quietness? (It sounds calm, gentle, peaceful, sleepy.)

Winds on the mountain

The piece is in three sections, in each of which the dynamics change. The dynamics include: **p** quiet; **pp** very quiet; **f** loud;

What you will need

🔘 12-14)))   📀 13

< crescendo (getting louder) > diminuendo (getting quieter).

Familiarise the children with these dynamic markings (printout 13), and ask them to indicate on the blank chart on the printout, the dynamic markings they would choose for each section and section ending.

Discuss their choices. Talk about the changes of dynamic within each section, and compare and contrast the sections with each other. (They may notice more detail than indicated in the completed chart below.)

first section	second section	third section
p **pp**	**f**	**pp**
first section ending	second section ending	third section ending
< > <	>	>

ASSESSMENT GUIDANCE

Can the children:

★ respond to changes of dynamics in music?

★ identify the changes of dynamics in music?

★ control instruments to make changes in dynamics?

★ use musical vocabulary and symbols to describe changes in dynamics?

Tempo introduction

• • • fast • • • • slow • • • • getting faster • • • • getting slower • •

ABOUT THE STARTER ACTIVITY
Traffic lights [WB] – a game, in which the children explore playing untuned percussion instruments at a variety of speeds, using visual signals.

WHAT YOU NEED TO KNOW ABOUT TEMPO

★ In music, the word for speed is tempo.

★ Music can be performed at varying speeds; we can sing a song slowly or quickly, or at any speed in between.

★ Whole sections of music often have a constant tempo throughout, neither speeding up nor slowing down. In other cases, music may progressively speed up throughout, or slow down throughout.

What you will need

 WB 5   14

• Printout of the traffic light cards. [WB]

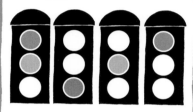

• Selection of untuned percussion instruments (drums, claves, maracas) – one per child.

• Recording equipment.

Traffic lights

1. Discuss with the children the sequence of colours in a set of traffic lights as shown on the printout.

2. Now explain to the children that they may play whatever they like on their instruments (eg a beat or a rhythmic pattern) but that it must be at a speed appropriate to the traffic signals.

3. To play the game, one child will be the conductor and will choose when to hold up the cards one at a time in sequence (it may help to number the back of the cards). The conductor may fine anyone who fails to slow down and stop by asking them to miss one turn!

4. Play these variations on the game to give the children practice in listening to each other.

Two conductors – two groups
The groups have contrasting instruments (eg wood/metal; shaken/tapped). Each conductor starts and stops their group independently.

Questions you might ask

• When did each group change speed?

• Which group speeded up first?

• Which group stopped first?

One at a time – small group
This time the conductor shows the first card to the children one at a time, in any order before going on to the next card.

Questions you might ask

• Who was the last person to play fast?

• Who was the last to stop?

No conductor – no signals
In a small group, the players try to make their playing conform to a common tempo as if they were in heavy traffic and had to avoid bumping into one another. The children will need to listen carefully to each other in order to accelerate and slow down together.

Questions you might ask

• Did you keep moving at the same speed?

• What would help you to do this better? (Watching each other as well as listening carefully; changing speed gradually; keeping in control.)

Teaching tip
The game can be played in small groups or with the whole class. Record the children playing to aid their discussion afterwards.

Tempo Winds on the mountain

• • • fast • • • • slow • • • • getting faster • • • • getting slower • •

WHAT YOU NEED TO KNOW ABOUT WINDS ON THE MOUNTAIN

★ *Winds on the mountain* is an instrumental piece based on a traditional South American melody.

★ It is performed by the British-based instrumental group, *Incantation*.

★ Change of tempo is a characteristic feature of many types of South American music. Sometimes a piece will consist of a short repeating melody, which gradually speeds up and increases in excitement. In **Winds on the mountain** the tempo changes from one section to the next: slow fast slow

★ Tempo structure of **Winds on the Mountain**:

first section – slow: the melody is played by large panpipes, then by flutes;

second section – fast: a change to double speed is signalled by the introduction of the bombo (drum); the panpipes and then flutes repeat the melody at the new tempo;

third section – slow; the melody drops back to the original tempo, this time played only by the panpipes.

★ The instruments heard in the piece are typically South American:

Sikus (see-kooss) – panpipes made from several reeds of graduated length bound together. The player blows across the top of the reed. The Indian people of the Andes mountains in Chile, Peru and Bolivia have played panpipes and flutes since the time of the Incas.

Quena (kay–nah) – a flute, most commonly made from bamboo but also from wood or bone.

Charango – the Indians originally used armadillo shells to make their own version of the guitars and mandolins introduced by the Spanish in the sixteenth century.

Bombo – a drum made from a hollowed out tree trunk covered with goatskin.

Cha'jchas (chah–jazz) – rattles made from goats' hooves strung together.

ABOUT THE ACTIVITIES

Wind dance – the children first explore then plan a wind dance using different speeds, directions and strengths of movement which correspond with the three sections of **Winds on the Mountain**: slow fast slow.

Wind dance

1. Explain to the children that the music they are going to hear – **Winds on the mountain** – is in three sections. Ask them to respond in movement as they listen to the first section (track 12).

Questions you might ask

• Does the music in this section change speed? (No.)

• How would you describe your movements? (Slow, floating, gentle, smooth, quiet, creeping.)

What you will need

 12-14))) 15

• A large space or hall in which the children can move freely.

· · · · fast · · · · · slow · · · · getting faster · · · · getting slower · ·

2. Now listen and move to the second section (track 13).

Questions you might ask

· What happened in the second section? (The music was faster.)

· How would you describe your movements in this section? (Energetic, lively, stepping, happy, strong.

3. Listen and move to the third section (track 14).

Questions you might ask

· How would you describe your movements this time? (They were similar to those in the first section.)

· How would you describe the speeds of the three sections? (Slow, fast, slow.)

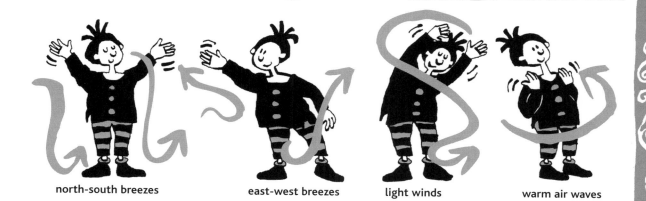

north-south breezes   east-west breezes   light winds   warm air waves

headwinds   cross winds   gales   gusts

Teaching tip

The ideas for movement are suggestions only – the children should preferably find their own.

When the wind dance is complete, perform it in assembly or for another class.

Printout 15 provides an illustration of the instruments.

4. Now collect together all the movement ideas for each section and decide with the children which to use in the dance.

5. Divide the class into groups and let each group choose and synchronise a pattern of movements. Let the groups organise the way in which they want to stand; for instance, they might stand in a circle for the first section and move in a line for the second.

Tempo Baris gede 'bandrangan'

• • • fast • • • • • slow • • • • • getting faster • • • • • getting slower • • •

WHAT YOU NEED TO KNOW ABOUT BARIS GEDE 'BANDRANGAN'

★ One of the main features of gamelan music (see also page 14) is the way in which the gamelan instruments play at different speeds according to their size and pitch.

★ This tempo relationship of the instruments to each other is maintained as the overall tempo speeds up and slows down, as it does in **Baris gede 'bandrangan'**.

ABOUT THE ACTIVITIES

Listen to *Gamelan* – the children listen to a simplified version of **Baris gede 'bandrangan'**, in which the tempos of the different instruments can be heard very clearly.

Listen to Baris gede 'bandrangan' – noticing overall changes in tempo.

Gamelan WB – performing a simplified version of **Baris gede 'bandrangan'**.

Listen to Gamelan

Help the children to focus on the low-, medium- and high-sounding instruments in turn as you ask them about their relative tempos. The drum signals the start and the overall speed, then is joined in turn by the lowest- to the highest-sounding instruments.

What you will need

(disc) 15)))

Questions you might ask

- Is the lowest-sounding instrument playing fast or slow? (Slow.)

- Can you describe the speed of the highest-sounding instrument? (It is fast, it is the same as the drum.)

- What do the other instruments do? (They play at two speeds in between the highest- and lowest-sounding instruments.)

Listen to Baris gede 'bandrangan'

Encourage the children to notice overall changes in tempo as they listen to these extracts from the beginning and ending of the piece.

The music begins with gongs playing a slow opening. The drum joins in to signal an increase in tempo as the first melody is repeated several times by the whole gamelan.

The ending shows how the tempo has increased again to create an even more exciting atmosphere. This is exaggerated by the very rapid drumming and cymbal playing.

At the very end, the music dramatically slows down as the original melody is played twice more.

What you will need

(disc) 10)))   (disc/pages) 21

Teaching tip

Refer to the printout (PO 21) of the gamelan instruments to help the children visualise what is happening in the music.

What you will need

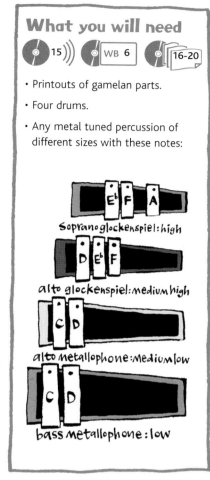

🔘 15))) 🔘 WB 6 🔘 16-20

- Printouts of gamelan parts.
- Four drums.
- Any metal tuned percussion of different sizes with these notes:

Eᵇ F A
Soprano glockenspiel: high

D Eᵇ F
alto glockenspiel: medium high

C D
alto metallophone: medium low

C D
bass metallophone: low

Teaching tip
When the groups are really confident, their lead drummer may speed up or slow down the overall tempo.

Gamelan

1. Remind the children of the *Dynamic drum* chant (page 16). This time the chant syllables fall on every drum beat:

• • • • • • • • • • • • • • • •

Ba -ris ge- de band-ran-gan, this ba- ris ge- de band-ran-gan, this

Remind the children of the actions from *Dynamic drum*, and perform the chant with a fourth action, eg tap knees:

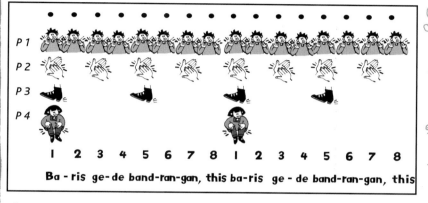

P 1
P 2
P 3
P 4

I 2 3 4 5 6 7 8 I 2 3 4 5 6 7 8

Ba - ris ge - de band-ran-gan, this ba-ris ge - de band-ran-gan, this

2. Divide the class into four groups, each with printouts of the four parts and instruments with the corresponding notes.

3. Each group appoints its own drummer and works out the patterns of the four different parts for themselves.

Each group decides for itself how to put the parts together, eg

– play the bass pattern first and then add the others one by one as on *Gamelan* (CD track 15); start in a different order; start all together.

– how many times each player with play;

– how to end.

The group's drummer will direct the tempo by tapping a steady beat.

Count	1	2	3	4	5	6	7	8	1	2	3	4	5	6	7	8
high	F	F	F	F	A	A	A	A	F	F	F	F	Eᵇ	Eᵇ	Eᵇ	Eᵇ
medium high	D		D		D		Eᵇ		D		Eᵇ		F		Eᵇ	
medium low	D				C				D				C			
low	C								D							
drum	ba – ris		– ge – de		band-ran-gan, this				ba – ris		– ge – de		band-ran-gan, this			

Tempo round up

• • • fast • • • • slow • • • • getting faster • • • • getting slower • •

When the children have completed the tempo activities in this section, give them opportunities to listen out for and comment on tempo in other sections. Here are some examples:

Dis long time, gal

Sections with contrasting tempos: explain that this music is a song which is repeated three times.

Questions you might ask

- Does this piece stay at the same speed all the way through or does it change speed? (It changes speed.)
- When does the music change speed? (The melody is slow the first time. The second and third times, the melody is fast.)

What you will need

💿 38)))

Rondeau

Music with a constant tempo throughout: explain that this music is based on a stately and elegant partner dance of the early eighteenth century. Ask the children to tap the pulse as they listen.

Questions you might ask

- Does the tempo stay the same, get faster or get slower during this piece? (It stays the same.)
- Can you think of a reason why the tempo needs to stay the same all the way through? (So that the dancers can step together in time with the music. If it got faster, the dancers might not be able to be so stately and elegant.)

What you will need

💿 41)))

ASSESSMENT GUIDANCE

Can the children:

★ respond to changes in tempo through movement?

★ play in several parts, maintaining a steady beat?

★ control instruments to make changes in tempo?

★ respond to signals indicating tempo made by a conductor?

★ recognise and describe changes in tempo using simple musical vocabulary?

Timbre introduction

• • •smooth • • •rough • • •hard • • •ringing • • • sparkling• • • shiny •

ABOUT THE STARTER ACTIVITY

Match up voices WB – in this game, the children explore their voices to produce different tone qualities (timbres).

What you will need

 WB 7 22

- Voices.
- Printout of the animal cards to display to the class. WB

Teaching tip

Play the game on different occasions, encouraging the children to be more imaginative each time they play it.

When the children can do all this confidently, ask them to say their names in the gap using a disguised voice. Everyone copies each solo voice, matching the sound as closely as possible. (You will have some inventive and hilarious results.)

WHAT YOU NEED TO KNOW ABOUT TIMBRE

★ Every sound has its own unique quality – this is timbre (taam-br).

★ Even though two sounds may be equally high or low, and may last the same length of time, we can discriminate between them if their timbres are different.

★ Everyone's voice has a timbre of its own, enabling us instantly to recognise friends and family by sound alone. Every different type of instrument has an individual timbre – think of the clear difference between the sound made by the wooden bars of a xylophone and the metal bars of a glockenspiel.

★ Within one instrument there can be a range of timbres, often affected by the way the instrument is played:

– a drum played with a beater sounds different from the same drum played with the hands;

– the string of a violin when it is played with the bow sounds very different from the same string plucked with the fingertip.

Match up voices

1. All together clap twice, then shake hands in the air twice to a steady beat:

clap   **clap**   **shake**   **shake**

2. When this is confident, show the children the printout of the fox card. Clap and shake again. This time when you show the fox card, everyone is silent. They count silently in their heads and can shake their hands silently but they must not clap until you hide the card again. Did everyone manage to keep in time? Practice until this is secure.

Show the other cards. Talk about the different sounds the duck, chicken and sheep would make and all try out some of the suggestions.

3. Now play the game. Shuffle the animal cards. Stand in a circle and establish the 'clap clap, shake shake' pattern. During the claps, show the first animal card to the first child in the circle, who makes the appropriate sound while the others shake their hands in the air. After the next set of claps, everyone copies the first child's animal sound. Show the next card to the second child, and so on round the circle.

At any time you can show the fox card, and everyone must keep the pattern going silently in their heads until the fox goes away.

Timbre La Volta

• • •smooth • • • rough • • • hard • • • ringing • • • sparkling • • • shiny •

WHAT YOU NEED TO KNOW ABOUT LA VOLTA

★ The volta was a court dance which became extremely popular for a short period at the end of the sixteenth century. It was only danced by the younger and more energetic ladies and gentlemen (including Queen Elizabeth I), because it contains high jumps and turns by both partners as well as a move in which the woman is lifted and turns in the air. The name of the dance (from the Spanish, voltear, to throw up in the air) refers to these moves.

★ Because the melody for the dance would have been played by whatever instruments happened to be available, the timbres changed accordingly. The children will compare two versions of *La Volta* and hear how the same melody, played at the same speed and on the same notes, sounds different because it is played on different instruments.

★ In the first version of the music for the dance (track 16), a violin plays the melody, accompanied by a lute and a viol. The lute and the viol repeatedly play the same notes throughout, which is a form of accompaniment called a drone.

★ The recorder plays the melody in the second version (track 17), accompanied by a harpsichord repeating a pattern of three different notes – an ostinato.

Lute – a many-stringed instrument used extensively in Elizabethan times. The strings are plucked with the fingertips.

Viol – one of a family of bowed string instruments of varying sizes. The violin and viol families developed at around the same time in the early 1500s, but the viol family dropped out of popularity 250 years later.

Violin – basically the same instrument then as it is now – a four-stringed instrument, played with a bow.

Harpsichord – a keyboard instrument which predates the modern piano. The strings are plucked by quills rather than being struck by hammers as in the case of the piano.

Recorder – very much the same instrument as today's, the recorder was very popular in Elizabethan households.

ABOUT THE ACTIVITIES

Listen to *La Volta* – as they listen, the children complete a table which shows the instrumentation of two versions of *La Volta*.

***La Volta* melody – first phrase** WB – in groups, the children learn to play a simplified version of *La Volta* melody.

***La Volta* melody – complete** WB – learning the complete *La Volta* melody.

***La Volta* drones** – devising accompaniments using drones on a variety of instruments.

***La Volta* ostinatos** – devising accompaniments using ostinatos on a variety of instruments.

***La Volta* arrangement** – choosing and combining instrumental timbres for a performance of *La Volta*.

lute

Viol

Violin

harpsichord

recorder

What you will need

 16-17))) 23-24

• A printout of the chart for each child.

Teaching tip

To help the children visualise what they are hearing, you may like to refer them to printout 23 which shows the instruments.

Listen to La Volta

As they listen to *La Volta*, the children compare the two versions by completing the printout chart as below.

La Volta	Same	Similar	Different
Melody (tune)	✔		
Tempo (speed)	✔		
Dynamics (loud/quiet)		✔	
Melody instruments			✔
Accompaniment instruments			✔

Questions you might ask

• Which instrument played the melody in each version? (Violin then the recorder.)

• Can you describe the accompaniment in each version? (In the first a string instrument, lute, was strummed like a guitar. The rhythm changed but the same notes were played all the way through – a drone. In the second, we heard a repeating pattern of three notes on the harpsichord – an ostinato. Sometimes the harpsichord copied the recorder's melody.)

What you will need

 18))) WB 8 24

• Printout of the simplified melody for each child. WB

• Photocopies of the staff notation of the melody (inside back cover) for music readers.

• A variety of tuned instruments such as recorders, xylophones, keyboards, violin.

La Volta melody I - first phrase

I. Teach the whole class the first phrase of melody 1 (below). This is a simplified version of *La Volta*. Sing it to the letter names of the notes. When it is secure, divide into two groups. Group 1 quietly tap knees and say the count, 1 2 3, 1 2 3, etc. Group 2 sings the melody.

2. Select a group of children to rehearse playing the first phrase on any of the suggested instruments. When this is secure, invite the group to play while the others sing it.

First phrase

									D		
B			B		B						
	A						A				
		G						G			
1	2	3	1	2	3	1	2	3	1	2	3

Timbre La Volta

• • • smooth • • • rough • • • hard • • • ringing • • • sparkling • • • shiny •

La Volta melody 1 + 2

1. Teach the class the second melody phrase (below) of *La Volta*, singing it to the letter names of the notes as before. When it is secure, divide into two groups again. Group 1 quietly tap knees and say the count, 1 2 3, 1 2 3, etc. Group 2 sings the melody.

2. Select a group of children to rehearse playing the second phrase on any of the suggested instruments. When this is secure, invite the group to play phrase 1 (previous page) and 2 while the others sing them.

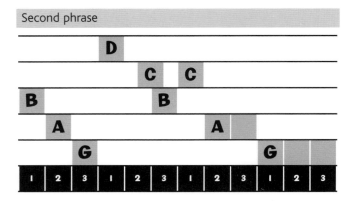

3. Continue by teaching the two phrases of melody 2 in the same way.

What you will need

 18 WB 8 25-26

• Printout of the simplified melody for each child. WB

• Photocopies of the staff notation of the melody (inside back cover) for music readers.

• Melody instruments from the previous activity.

Teaching tip

Use the melodies in whichever way suits your children's abilities best. They might simply keep repeating the first phrase of melody 1 throughout. More able children will manage an arrangement such as that on the recording, in which melody 1 is repeated several times, then melody 2 is repeated, and finally melody 1 returns.

La Volta drones

1. Show the children the drone printout and demonstrate each of the suggested drones while they quietly tap the pulse on their knees or say the count.

Chime bars – strike both bars together on count 1;

Keyboard – play notes D and G together on count 1;

Guitar – strum the chord of G on every count;

Glockenspiel – play G, or G and D together on each count.

2. Give individuals turns to play the drones one at a time, while the other children continue the pulse or the quiet count – or sing the melody.

3. When this is secure, select a small group to play the drones as an accompaniment to a group playing the melody on instruments while the others tap, count or sing the melody.

Teaching tip

The drone and ostinato parts on the printout each last as long as one melody phrase – repeat as required for your arrangement.

What you will need

 19 27

• Printouts of the drone card to display to the class and for each player.

• Guitars (chord G); chime bars, glockenspiels, keyboards, notes G and D:

• • • smooth • • • rough • • • hard • • • ringing • • • sparkling • • • shiny •

What you will need

- Printouts of the ostinato card to display to the class and for each player.
- Tambours, drums, Indian bells, tambourines, xylophone:

Teaching tip

Listen to sample performances of the melody, drones and ostinatos on tracks 19 and 20.

What you will need

- Printouts of the melody, drone and ostinatos cards for each player.
- Instruments for playing the melody, drones and ostinatos.
- Recording equipment.

La Volta ostinatos

1. Show the children the ostinato printout and demonstrate each of the suggested ostinatos while they quietly tap the pulse on their knees or say the count. They may find it helpful to repeat the suggested word rhythms quietly as they play:

Tambour/drum:

1	2	3	1	2	3
Vol	-	ta	Vol	-	ta

Tambourine:

1	2	3	1	2	3
Jump			La	Vol -	ta

Indian bells:

1	2	3	1	2	3
Lift		and	turn		

Xylophone – play:

1	2	3	1	2	3
G	D	G'	G	D	G'

2. Give individuals turns to play the ostinatos one at a time, while the other children continue the pulse or the quiet count – or sing the melody.

3. When this is secure, select a small group to play the ostinatos as an accompaniment to a group playing the melody on instruments while the others tap, count or sing the melody.

La Volta arrangement

1. Divide the class into small groups, each with:

Melody players;

Drone players;

Ostinato players.

2. The drone and ostinato players select and try out different combinations of instruments and consider their suitability for accompanying the melody instruments in their group.

They may:

– play any or all drones;

– play any or all ostinatos;

– play a mixture of drones and ostinatos;

– make up their own ostinato patterns.

3. Encourage the children to consider carefully the effect of different combinations of timbres by recording and listening to their choices.

4. When each group has completed an arrangement of the piece, share it with the rest of the class, comparing the timbre effects created by their choices of instrument and accompaniments.

Timbre Tomorrow the fox
• • • smooth • • • rough • • • hard • • • ringing • • • sparkling • • • shiny •

WHAT YOU NEED TO KNOW ABOUT TOMORROW THE FOX

★ Composer: Thomas Ravenscroft (c1590 – c1635).

★ This song dates from the time of Elizabeth I, although its melody, *Trenchmore*, was written in Henry VIII's time.

★ It was common at this time to write new words to existing popular tunes already familiar to the public.

★ In 1609, Ravenscroft published two of the earliest collections of English printed songs. Many of these were rounds and included probably the first printed version of *Three blind mice*.

★ Although he was a learned church musician, Ravenscroft was determined to write music for all tastes: for 'court, city and country'. Another more practical reason for publishing collections of popular and part-songs was that he was unable to make a living from church music alone.

★ In *Tomorrow the fox*, there are many contrasts of timbre. The piece starts with unaccompanied voices and the timbres of the individual female and male voices can clearly be heard. This is followed by a rousing instrumental section performed here on Elizabethan string and wind instruments which have a particularly 'rustic' timbre.

The piece continues, alternating instrumental sections with voices and instruments combined, and every so often the instruments suddenly stop and the voices are heard alone again.

★ *Tomorrow the fox* contrasts strongly with **La Volta**, which is typical of the more elegant court music of the same period. The song would have been performed in taverns and outdoors, so the voices are accompanied by instruments which have a particularly powerful timbre:

Tambourine – originally a Middle Eastern instrument, and little changed in 800 years, it was introduced into Europe during medieval times.

Cittern (sih-tern) – a pear-shaped instrument with metal strings which are plucked or strummed.

Bass curtal (kuhr-tal) – a double reed wind instrument similar to the bassoon.

Treble rebec (reh-bek) – a small pear-shaped, bowed string instrument used particularly for song and dance music (can be heard playing the melody in the instrumental sections).

ABOUT THE ACTIVITIES

Match up memory WB – a sound matching game for individuals, groups or the whole class.

Tomorrow the fox song – learning the song.

Scrap band – exploring and distinguishing between the timbres of a range of recycled sound-makers.

Listen to Scrap band – discriminating between the timbres of different materials.

Listen to *Tomorrow the fox* – focusing on timbres.

***Tomorrow the fox* finale** – performing the song and selecting three instrumental timbres to represent the hen, lamb and duck.

tambourine   Cittern   bass curtal   treble rebec

 • • • smooth • • • rough • • • hard • • • ringing • • • sparkling • • • shiny •

What you will need

21-24))) WB 9 29-30

• Printouts of the instrument strips and an answer chart for each child. WB

Teaching tip

The children will hear each instrument strip, then four questions in which one instrument from the strip is missing. Answers – the missing instruments are:

Track 21 – Question 1 Cow bell. 2 Tulip block. 3 Tambour. 4 Castanet.

Track 22 – 1 Recorder. 2 Lute. 3 Violin. 4 Harpsichord.

Track 23 – 1 Panpipes. 2 Tin whistle. 3 Mouth harp. 4 Tamboura.

Track 24 – 1 Curtal. 2 Tambourine. 3 Rebec. 4 Cittern.

What you will need

 25-26))) 31

• Printouts of the song sheet for everyone.

Teaching tip

The first verse and chorus are given on track 25 with gaps after each line for the children to copy.

Track 26 is a backing track for singing along to.

Staff notation is given at the back of the book for music readers.

Match up memory

1. Together, listen to each track in turn – the instruments are heard in the order in which they appear on the strips. Identify the name and type of instrument together, eg *Tomorrow the fox* instruments:

rebec   cittern   tambourine   bass curtal

Questions you might ask

• Which instrument is struck? (Tambourine). Which is blown? (Bass curtal.) How are the other two instruments played? (The rebec is played with a bow like a violin; the cittern is strummed like a guitar.)

2. Individually, in small groups, or as a class, listen to the quiz questions on each track. Draw a picture or write the name of the missing instrument in the answer chart.

Tomorrow the fox song

1. Teach the song to the class.

Verse 1   **Tomorrow the fox will come to town,**
Keep! keep! keep! keep! keep!
Tomorrow the fox will come to town,
Oh, keep you all well there.

Chorus   **I must desire you neighbours all**
To hallow the fox out of the hall,
And cry as loud as you can call:
Woop! woop! woop! woop! woop!
And cry as loud as you can call,
Oh, keep you all well there.

Verse 2   **He'll steal the hen e'en from the pen!**
Keep! keep! keep! keep! keep!
He'll steal the hen e'en from the pen!
Oh, keep you all well there.

Verse 3   **He'll steal the lamb e'en from the dam!**
Keep! keep! keep! ...

Verse 4   **He'll steal the duck e'en from the brook!**
Keep! keep! keep! ...

Timbre Tomorrow the fox

• • • smooth • • • rough • • • hard • • • ringing • • • sparkling • • • shiny •

Scrap band

1. Divide the class into four groups and allocate to each group one of the four sets of recycled sound-makers.

2. All chant the chorus of **Tomorrow the fox** while tapping the rhythm of the words on your knees:

I must   de - sire   you neigh-bours all...

3. Now all play the rhythm of the chorus words on their sound-makers.

Questions you might ask

• What did it sound like when we all played together? (You will get a mixture of responses: some may have liked the loudness, others may not have been able to hear their own sound.)

4. Sing this new version of the song, which groups the instruments into their different materials. Each group takes their turn to play the rhythm of the chorus words, while the others quietly tap the rhythm on their knees. Everyone sings the 'Woop woop' line out loud together:

Verse 1   **Tomorrow the band will come to town,**
          Keep! keep! keep! keep! keep!
          Tomorrow the band will come to town,
          Oh, keep your paper there.

          All paper instruments play the chorus rhythm.

Chorus   x x   x x   x x   x x
          x x x x   x x   x x
          x x   x x   x x   x x

All   **Woop! woop! woop! woop! woop!**
          x x   x x x x   x x
          x x   x x x   x

Verse 2   **Tomorrow the band will come to town...**
          ...Oh, keep your timber there.

          All timber instruments play the chorus rhythm.

Verse 3   **Tomorrow the band will come to town...**
          ...Oh, keep your metal there.

          All metal instruments play the chorus rhythm.

Verse 4   **Tomorrow the band will come to town...**
          ...Oh, keep your plastic there.

          All plastic instruments play the chorus rhythm.

What you will need

 26-27))) 31

• A sound-maker for each child from a collection of four clean, recycled materials, eg

  paper: newspaper, tissue paper, crinkly wrapping paper;

  wood: off-cuts of wood, chopsticks, wooden spoons, twigs;

  plastic: pots, spoons and tubs;

  metal: spoons, cans, washers, biscuit tins.

• A copy of the song sheet for everyone.

Teaching tip
Play along with backing track 26 or with track 27, which is a performance of the song.

Questions you might ask

• Which of our scrap band instruments made the quietest sounds? Which made the loudest? Which did you like best?

• Can you think of any other objects we could use to create different timbres? (Tables, chairs, cutlery, cardboard boxes, wastepaper bins, dustbin lids.)

• • • smooth • • • rough • • • hard • • • ringing • • • sparkling • • • shiny •

What you will need

Listen to Scrap band

Play the performance track of *Scrap band*. Can the children identify the materials and describe how they think the sounds might be made? (paper – newspaper torn rhythmically, tissue paper scrunched; wood – thick sticks rubbed together, one stick tapped with another; metal – bolts tapped together, radiator tapped with spoon; plastic – ridged bottle scraped, two bottles tapped together.)

What you will need

Listen to Tomorrow the fox

Questions you might ask

- What do you hear in the first verse and chorus of this song? (Male and female voices – no instruments.)

- When the instruments play first, are they alone or playing with the voices? (Alone – they play a link after the chorus.)

- Can you describe the sounds of any of the instruments and say how they might be played? (The children should be able to pick out a high-pitched, bowed string instrument, a gruff bass line played by a blown instrument, and a tambourine.)

Teaching tip
Use the printout picture of the instruments as a visual reference for the children if you wish.

What you will need

• A large selection of percussion instruments

• Printout of *Tomorrow the fox* song sheet.

Tomorrow the fox finale

1. Revise singing the song, then divide into three groups. Allocate the hen, lamb and duck characters – one to each group.

2. With each group in turn, discuss and practise a vocal timbre to suit their creature.

3. When this is agreed, ask the groups in turn to select instruments with suitable timbres for their creatures. Give the groups practice in singing the chorus using their chosen vocal timbre while playing its rhythm on the chosen instruments – the group may like to divide into singers and players.

4. Together create a score to remind everyone when they will sing and play, eg:

Teaching tip
Use backing track 26 for extra accompaniment support if you wish.

All: Verse **Hens: Chorus** **All: Verse** **Sheep: Chorus** **All: Verse** **Ducks: Chorus**

Timbre round up

• • • smooth • • • rough • • • hard • • • ringing • • • sparkling • • • shiny •

When the children have completed the timbre activities in this section, give them opportunities to listen out for and comment on timbre in other sections. Here are some examples:

Kartal

What you will need

45)))

Questions you might ask

- What material do you think the instrument is made of? (Wood.)
- How do you think the sound is being made? (The pieces of wood are tapped together - see page 58.)
- Are there any classroom instruments we could use to make a similar sound? (Claves, castanets, wood block or table top and wooden sticks.)

Winds on the mountain

The children hear typical South American instruments of contrasting and distinctive timbres (see page 20).

What you will need

12-14)))

Questions you might ask

- How do you think the first two instruments are played? (The first is blown, the second has strings which are strummed with the fingers.)
- Which new instruments can you hear in the fast section? (Drums and rattles.)

Five pieces for orchestra, no 1

The composer of this very short piece, Webern, has used instruments of the orchestra in an unusual way which highlights their individual timbres so that it is possible to hear their different tone qualities very clearly.

What you will need

29)))

Questions you might ask

- Can you identify any of the instruments? (Flute, glockenspiel, harp, trumpet, violin and clarinet.)

ASSESSMENT GUIDANCE

Can the children:

★ control their voices to produce a variety of different timbres?

★ recognise that different instruments have different timbres?

★ discriminate between and identify musical instruments by their timbre?

★ select instruments to combine a variety of different timbres?

★ describe timbres using musical and descriptive vocabulary?

Texture introduction

• • • thin • • thick • • solo • • chorus • • one sound • • several sounds • •

ABOUT THE STARTER ACTIVITY

One two many – an improvisation game for the children to explore different musical textures on voices and body percussion.

WHAT YOU NEED TO KNOW ABOUT TEXTURE

★ Sounds can be used singly or in any variety of combinations – this is texture.

★ Texture can be as thin as the sound of a solo voice or as thick as the sound of a large orchestra all playing together.

★ Often the texture changes within a piece of music, adding to the interest.

What you will need

◎ WB 10

• Voices and body percussion.

One two many

1. Ask each child in the class to choose a sound they can make with their voices, hands or bodies. Point to each child one by one as everyone listens to the different sounds. Explain that these are all single sounds, but that now you are going to combine them in different ways.

2. Choose a conductor to lead the class. The conductor stands where everyone can see and points to individuals, pairs, and the whole group, using these four signals:

 one person performs their chosen sound;

 two people perform their chosen sounds;

 everyone performs their sounds;

 all stop – silence.

Once signalled, each player continues their sound until the signal moves to someone else.

Teaching tip

Choose a theme, eg animals, transport, machines, ring tones, Choose another conductor to lead as the children improvise sounds to match the theme.

Questions you might ask

• What did you notice about the sounds we made? (Sometimes only one person was performing, sometimes two, or all of us.)

• What did it sound like when we were all performing? (Loud, busy, exciting.)

• What else made the music exciting? (Changing quickly between one, two and many players; watching and listening carefully for our turn.)

Texture Five pieces for orchestra, no 1

• • • thin • • thick • • solo • • chorus • • • one sound • • several sounds • • •

WHAT YOU NEED TO KNOW ABOUT FIVE PIECES FOR ORCHESTRA, NO 1

★ Composer: Anton Webern (born Vienna, 1883–1945).

★ Webern composed this set of five pieces in 1913, each one a miniature lasting a minute or less.

★ No 1 is titled 'Sehr ruhig und zart' – very calm and delicate. Webern uses tiny fragments of melody, chooses the instruments of his orchestra for their distinctive timbres, then weaves the sounds together in a very open texture. The composer, Stravinsky, a contemporary of Webern, likened his music to 'dazzling diamonds', and indeed Webern seems to treat each sound like a unique, precious gem.

★ Although written for orchestra, Piece No 1 is unusual in that the texture is very thin. At the beginning and end of the piece, instruments play the fragments of melody singly one after the other; the middle section has a very slightly thicker texture as the instruments briefly combine or overlap.

Beginning – the harp and (muted) trumpet, celeste, flute and glockenspiel play single sounds one after the other making a very thin texture.

Middle – this is made up of combinations of different sounds, making the texture slightly thicker.

End – glockenspiel, harp, flute, trumpet and finally celeste play one by one mirroring the very thin texture of the beginning.

Listen to *Five pieces for orchestra, no 1* – collecting and discussing first impressions of the music.

Night music sounds WB – preparing sounds for a piece of music with a musical texture similar to that created by Webern.

Night music WB – the music is performed.

Listen to *Five pieces for orchestra, no 1* – noticing the connections between the children's *Night music* performance and Webern's music.

First impressions – creating a new piece of music based on the children's first impressions of Webern's music.

Listen to Five pieces for orchestra, no 1

Listen several times with the children.

After they have heard the piece a few times, discuss their reactions to and ideas about the music. Collect together the words they use to describe the music and a list of any scenes they imagine as they listen.

Questions you might ask

- What mood was the music – calm, gentle, strong, exciting, mysterious, happy, lonely?

- Did you imagine any pictures or stories as you listened?

- What words would you use to describe the sounds?

What you will need

 29)))

Teaching tip

It may help the children to concentrate on listening if they close their eyes.

Keep the children's word and scene collection for the later activities.

• • • thin • • thick • • solo • • chorus • • one sound • • several sounds • •

Night music sounds

1. Display the Night music score where the whole class can see it.

2. Reading from left to right, notice how there are individual words at the beginning and end of the score, eg night, calm, sleep.

And notice how the middle section overlaps in a complex night scene.

3. Beginning and end

Choose eight children and allocate one child to each of the eight words – night, dark, quiet, cold, calm, still, peace and sleep. Each child will then select a sound which they think suggests their word. They will need time to try out different ideas on the instruments. When they are ready, listen together to the thin texture of each chosen sound played one after the other.

4. Middle

Divide the rest of the class into four small groups, to each of which is allocated one feature of the night scene:

1 **moon, stars and space**; 2 **trees**; 3 **water and reflections**; 4 **reeds**.

Within their groups, each child selects a sound which suggests their part of the picture, and then each group tries out combining and ordering the individual sounds into a texture of their choice for their part of the night scene.

What you will need

- A wide variety of instruments – enough for each child to choose one for its special sound quality. (The instruments below show the range you might aim for. Supplement with environmental sound-makers if necessary.)
- Printout of Night music score. WB

Teaching tip

The texture of the middle section is further developed by the conductor in performance (page 38).

Texture Five pieces for orchestra, no 1

• • • thin • • • thick • • solo • • chorus • • • one sound • • several sounds • •

Night music

1. Having prepared sounds in the previous activity, the children get into their groups again for the performance, in which the final texture of the piece takes shape. Display the *Night music* score.

2. Appoint a conductor, who will bring in the sounds by pointing to them on the score as the signal for the children to play:

   Beginning and end – sounds are played one by one as the conductor points to each word in turn;

   Middle – the conductor points to the parts of the night scene, which should be played separately or in combination. The conductor can bring groups in in different combinations, let them be heard once only, all together, and so on (there are many different texture options).

3. Record the result and discuss the textures with the children.

What you will need

 WB 11   32

- The instruments from the previous activity.
- Recording equipment.
- Printout of *Night music* score. WB

Teaching tip
Give other children turns to conduct alternative versions.

Listen to Five pieces for orchestra, no 1

Questions you might ask

• How is this music similar to our *Night music*? (All the sounds are quiet. Both pieces use a lot of different instruments. The instruments play only a few sounds each. The sounds are heard one by one at first, then several sounds together in the middle section, then one by one at the end.)

What you will need

29)))

First impressions

1. Remind the children of the words and scenes they collected when they listened to Webern's music for the first time.

2. Using one of the scenes suggested from the children's first impressions, create a new picture score. Use the picture as a plan for a new composition using the same structure:

   beginning and end – word sounds played singly,

   middle – central picture to represent sounds which can be played in different combinations.

   Use the new score to select instruments and sounds to create another performance. Record this new piece of music and compare it with the Webern and the children's *Night music* performance.

Questions you might ask

• What is similar about all three pieces? (The musical structure.)

• What is different about all three? (The instruments and sounds used, the mood, the dynamics or tempo.)

Texture Dis long time, gal

• • • thin • • thick • • solo • • chorus • • one sound • • several sounds • •

ABOUT THE ACTIVITIES

Dis long time gal **song** – learning the song on which the music is based.

Steel pan sort out – familiarising the children with the sound of the different steel pans.

One two many crows – playing a rhythm in a variety of musical textures using body percussion.

Listen to *Dis long time, gal* – recognising connections between *One two many* and *Dis long time, gal*.

Texture twist – recognising changes of texture in *Dis long time, gal*.

One two many crows with instruments – playing a rhythm in a variety of musical textures using untuned percussion.

A new twist – using the texture features from the arrangement of *Dis long time, gal* to make a new piece of music.

WHAT YOU NEED TO KNOW ABOUT DIS LONG TIME, GAL

★ *Dis long time gal* is a traditional Jamaican song.

★ This arrangement of the song was written for and performed by a junior school steel band.

★ A variety of musical textures are heard as sections of the band play singly and in combination.

First verse – the piece opens with the tenor pans playing the melody in unison (everyone playing the same notes) – a thin texture.

First chorus – the tenor pans are divided into two groups, one playing the melody, the other playing the melody shape on different notes.

Second verse: the bass pans play a very short section on their own, then the texture thickens as the cellos play the melody accompanied by the tenors playing decorative notes above.

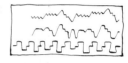

Second chorus: the same texture is maintained.

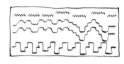

Third verse – the texture is further thickened by the addition of a drum kit which plays a short solo before the pans enter; the melody is played on tenors with tenors and cellos accompanying.

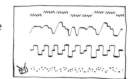

Third chorus – the same texture is maintained to the end.

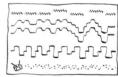

bass pans

tenor pans

cello pans

Texture Dis long time, gal

• • • thin • • • thick • • solo • • • chorus • • • one sound • • • several sounds • •

Dis long time, gal song

1. Teach the song:

> Verse 1   **Dis long time, gal, me never see yu,**
> **Come mek me hol your han.**
> **Dis long time, gal, me never see yu,**
> **Come mek me hol your han.**

> Chorus   **Peel head John Crow sid up on tree-top**
> **Pick off de blossom,**
> **Mek me hol your han, gal,**
> **Mek me hol your han.**

> Verse 2   **Dis long time, gal, me never see yu,**
> **Come mek we walk an talk...**

> Chorus   **Peel head John Crow...**

> Verse 3   **Dis long time, gal, me never see yu,**
> **Come mek we wheel an turn...**

> Chorus   **Peel head John Crow...**

What you will need

• Voices.

• Printouts of the song sheet.

Steel pan sort out

1. Display the printout of the steel band where everyone can see it.

Together, identify the three groups of pans and the physical differences between them.

What you will need

• Printout of the steel band picture to display to the class.

Questions you might ask

• Which pans are the largest? (The bass pans.)

• Which are the smallest? (The tenor pans.)

• Which pans would you expect to make the lowest-sounding notes? (The largest; the bass pans.)

• Which would you expect to make the highest-sounding notes? (The smallest; the tenor pans.)

• What kind of sounds would you expect the cello pans to make? (A medium sound; between high-sounding and low-sounding.)

2. Play *Steel pan sort*, CD track 31, and ask the children if they recognise the melody. (**Dis long time, gal**.)

3. Now play all the *Steel pan sort out* tracks, 31-35.

Questions you might ask

• When can you hear the melody played on its own? (In tracks 31 and 33.)

• Which pans do you think played in these two tracks? (Tenors in track 31; cellos in track 33.)

• Which pans do you think played each time, and how do you know? (The tenors played first; they are the smallest and make the highest sound. The bass pans played last; they are the biggest and make the deepest sound. The cellos played the melody after the tenors; they played it faster; the cellos played with the basses in one of the tracks.)

Teaching tip

The steel pans are heard in this order:

Track 31 – the tenor pans play the verse melody slowly.

Track 32 – the tenors divide into two parts to play the chorus melody and a part which moves in parallel with it.

Track 33 – the cellos are heard playing the melody.

Track 34 – the bass pans begin, joined by the tenors and cellos, playing an accompaniment to the melody which is not heard.

Track 35 – the bass pans play the bass line alone.

The children may need to listen to the extracts several times in order to answer the questions.

• • • thin • • thick • • solo • • chorus • • one sound • • several sounds • •

What you will need

◎ 36-37)))

One two many crows

1. Together chant these words from *Dis long time, gal*:

| Peel | head | John | Crow |

| Sid | up | | on | tree | - | top |

2. Practise clapping the rhythm with the children until they can clap it from memory without the words.

3. Choose a conductor and remind the class of the *One two many* signals they used in the starter activity:

 one person performs

 two people perform

 everyone performs

 all stop – silence

Teaching tip

Track 36 gives the chant, and track 37 demonstrates the game with vocal signals.

Ensure that the children understand the signals and give them plenty of practice by leading the game yourself initially.
– always start with signal 1, then use the signals in any order, ending with the stop signal.
– point at individual players when using signals 1 and 2.
– once signalled to, the players keep repeating the rhythm until the signal moves to someone else.

Each player performs the rhythm, *Peel head John Crow sid up on tree-top*, using their own choice of vocal or body percussion. As before, they begin when signalled and continue until the signal moves to another player:

ch ch ch ch chch chch ch

4. After a round of the game, discuss the variety of textures.

Questions you might ask

• Who played on their own – a solo?

• When two people played together, were they using different body sounds or the same to play the rhythm?

• What was the effect when the whole group played together? (It was much louder, there were lots of different sounds – stamping, clapping, clicking, tapping – all playing the rhythm at once.)

• Which texture was the thinnest? (The solo.)

• Which was the thickest? (When everyone joined in.)

Texture Dis long time, gal

• • • thin • • thick • • solo • • chorus • • • one sound • • several sounds • •

Listen to Dis long time, gal

Questions you might ask

• How is the texture of this piece similar to that of the game we played? (At first we heard one melody, then there were two playing together. When the melody was repeated there were lots of instruments playing.)

• When you hear two parts playing the melody, are they playing the same rhythm or do they have different rhythms? (The same.)

• Can you hear two different steel pans playing a different rhythm from each other? (Yes, the cellos and basses; the tenors and basses; the cellos and tenors.)

What you will need

 38)))   35

• Printout of the steel band picture to display to the class.

Texture twist

1. Play *Dis long time, gal* and ask the children to listen with closed eyes, indicating by a show of hands, the beginning of each new verse and chorus.

2. Display the texture strips where the whole class can see them. Discuss each strip with the class, noticing the way the steel band parts have been notated using simple line drawings of the shape of each part.

What you will need

 38)))   36

• Printouts of the texture strips to display to the class.

Questions you might ask

• Which strip shows the tenors playing the melody in unison? (Strip 1.)

• In which strip do the bass pans play on their own first? (Strip 3.)

• Which strip shows the drum kit playing first? (Strip 5.)

Teaching tip

Let individual children play the game. You will need to give them access to a CD player or a computer and headphones.

3. Play the first verse and chorus of *Dis long time, gal*. Follow the shape of the melody with a pointer and help the children recognise how the line drawing of the verse melody and chorus melody differ. Continue matching up the texture strips with the verses and choruses on the recording.

4. Now jumble the strips, and as the class listens to the recording again, ask individuals to indicate which strip is currently being played. Was the order correct? Listen again to check.

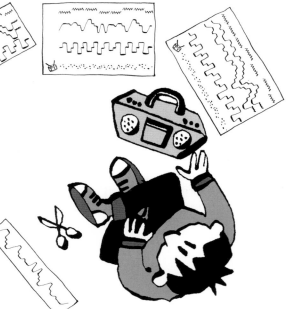

• • • thin • • thick • • solo • • chorus • • one sound • • several sounds • •

What you will need

• A selection of untuned percussion instruments.

One two many crows with instruments

1. Explain that you are going to play *One two many* again, but that this time you will be using instruments on which to play the rhythm, eg

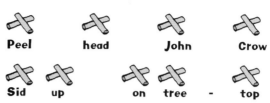

Peel	head	John	Crow

| Sid | up | on | tree | - | top |

2. Encourage the conductors to think about interesting textures of sounds they might achieve as they choose one, two, or all of the players.

3. As before, discuss the different sequences of textures which are produced in each game as the conductors use the signals in different ways.

4. As the children become confident with the game, each new conductor may also choose a new rhythm, eg

long   time,   gal, me never see yu

or

come   mek   me hol   your   han

Teaching tip

If you have enough instruments, give one per child. If not, distribute what you have and let the children take turns using instruments or body percussion.

A new twist

1. Divide the class into small groups, each with a set of texture strips and a selection of instruments.

2. Each group makes up a new piece of music using the texture strips as their starting point:

– they may order the strips any way they like;

– they may turn them upside down to make a new melodic shape;

– they may reinterpret the line notation to make up new parts;

– they may use a known melody, arrange it, and write their own line notation and their own texture strips.

What you will need

• Printouts of sets of texture strips – one set for each group.

• Different types of melody instrument, eg recorder, kazoo, xylophone, keyboard, swanee whistle.

• Some untuned percussion instruments.

Texture round up

When the children have completed the texture activities in this section, give them opportunities to listen out for and comment on texture in other sections. Here are some examples:

Didlan

Ask the children to notice how the texture changes. (It starts with a single voice, which is joined by a second and then by a third. Later in the piece, the texture thickens again as more voice parts are added.

What you will need
39

Tomorrow the fox

Questions you might ask

• What do you hear at the beginning of this piece? (Singing; a female voice and male voices singing together.)

• There are three main textures in this piece. Can you say what they are? (Voices only, instruments only, and voices with instruments.)

What you will need
28   37

Show the children the printout of the texture plan of the music, and follow it together as you listen to the track again.

Unsquare dance

The sounds which make up the texture are hand clapping, double bass, piano, and tapping with sticks on the rim of a drum. As the music moves through four sections, the combination of these sounds changes. On the printouts of the texture chart, the children tick which sounds they hear in each section. They may need to listen several times. Answer:

What you will need
3   38

	Section 1	Section 2	Section 3	Section 4
Bass drum			✔	
Grand piano		✔		✔
Clapping	✔	✔	✔	
Double bass	✔	✔	✔	

ASSESSMENT GUIDANCE

Can the children:

★ recognise and discriminate between changing textures in music?

★ perform in response to signals indicating different textures?

★ organise sounds to create a variety of different musical textures?

★ understand how different textures can produce different musical effects?

★ describe different musical textures, including solo and duet?

Pitch introduction

• • • high low • • getting higher • • getting lower • • staying the same • •

ABOUT THE STARTER ACTIVITY

Pitch in WB – exploring vocal ranges by singing a well-known song, starting at a different pitch each time: low, medium and high.

WHAT YOU NEED TO KNOW ABOUT PITCH

★ Sounds in music can range from low to high – this is what is referred to as pitch.

★ Our voices can produce more than one pitch, but the total range of notes we can sing comfortably is determined by whether we are male or female, and by our age. The ranges of the voice are given special names. The most common are:

soprano – high (children and women)

alto – medium to high (children, women and some men)

tenor – medium (men)

bass – low (men)

★ As a general rule, larger instruments produce lower pitches. For example, a large drum will make a lower sound than a small drum of a similar type.

What you will need

• Voices.

• Chime bars A, E B. WB
(If chime bars are not available, use any pitched instrument, eg piano – A below middle C, E and B above.)

Pitch in

1. Choose a simple tune that everyone knows well, eg *Frère Jacques*, and ensure that the whole class is familiar with it by singing it together.

2. Now ask the children to suggest some nonsense sounds they can sing instead of the words, eg

(Frè - re   Jac - ques...)   (Frè - re   Jac - ques...)

zee zee zee   zee...   or   **da   da   da   dum...**

3. Strike the middle chime bar, E, and sing the song to the new nonsense syllables, using this as the starting note.

4. Repeat, this time starting on the highest-sounding bar, B.

5. Sing at the middle pitch again, then try the lowest-sounding bar, A.

Questions you might ask

• Which version sounded highest/lowest?

• Was it easy to sing all three ways – high, medium and low?

• If not, which one was most comfortable for our voices? (Individual children may have different preferences.)

Pitch Didlan

• • • high low • • getting higher • • getting lower • • staying the same • •

WHAT YOU NEED TO KNOW ABOUT DIDLAN

★ *Didlan* is an arrangement of the Welsh folk song, *The Ash Grove*.

★ It is performed and was arranged by Plethyn (pleh-thin), a Welsh folk group.

★ The arrangement is for three voices: one female (soprano), and two male (tenor and bass).

★ The performers do not sing the traditional words, but instead sing nonsense words, 'dee dee dee diddle', a technique used variously in many traditional cultures, and sometimes called diddling.

★ The arrangement shows off the contrast between the soprano, tenor and bass voices of the group:

soprano – the melody is sung by the female singer all the way through the piece. The children will hear this voice alone first;

tenor – the higher of the two male voices, the tenor, joins in singing a harmony part under the melody;

bass – this is followed by the lowest voice, the bass, adding a bass part underneath the two upper parts.

As the music continues, more parts are added by recording the singers' own voices together with the original three parts.

ABOUT THE ACTIVITIES

Listen to *Didlan* – recognising the contrasts in pitch between the singing voices.

Singing snakes and ladders WB – a game which gives the children the opportunity to use their voices at different pitches in a variety of ways.

Listen to Didlan

Explain to the children that they will hear a song. The words of the song will be nonsense words.

Questions you might ask

• What do you hear first? (A woman's voice.)

• Do you hear any instruments? (No.)

• How many other singers can you hear? (Two men.)

• Who has the highest voice? (The first singer, the woman.)

• Whose voice is lowest? (The third singer's.)

What you will need

🔘 35)))

• • • high low • • getting higher • • getting lower • • staying the same • •

What you will need

- A printout of the game board to display to the class. WB
- One die.
- Two xylophones with these notes (to help pitch the notes for squares 3 and 13):

Singing snakes and ladders

1. To start the game, choose a song together and sing it in your normal voices at a comfortable pitch.

2. Now choose one of the children to throw the die to move to a new square.

3. Follow the instructions on each new square you land on, using your voices to make the sounds indicated.

Teaching tip

Later, the game can be played in small groups or pairs.
Version 1 – on each square do something with the pitch of your voices.
Version 2 – play each task on a melody instrument, eg xylophone or recorder instead of singing it.

Sample extract from Singing Snakes and Ladders (see printout 39-40 and WB activity)

Pitch Stamping tubes

• • • high low • • getting higher • • getting lower • • staying the same • •

WHAT YOU NEED TO KNOW ABOUT STAMPING TUBES

★ This piece of music is from the Solomon Islands in the Pacific Ocean.

★ In the Solomon Islands, 'bamboos of the ground' – stamping tubes – are played for entertainment.

★ Each bamboo tube is a different length and diameter and so produces a different musical pitch.

★ The musicians hold two tubes in each hand and strike the open ends on a large, smooth stone.

★ In this piece, three young women play a total of twelve stamping tubes to create an exciting effect of patterns in which the combinations of pitches can clearly be heard.

ABOUT THE ACTIVITIES

Tapping tubes – investigating the relationship between the length and the pitch of different tubes.

Tapping tube trio– performing a piece of tapping tube music using a simple form of notation.

Pitch walls WB – making up a simple pattern of pitches and notating them on pitch walls; playing the patterns using instruments of three contrasting pitches: high, medium and low.

Pitch buildings WB – creating whole pieces of music out of the pitch walls.

Tapping tubes

1. Choose three tubes of different length. Give one tube and one tapper each to three children.

2. Ask each child in turn to tap one end of their tube while the rest of the class listen carefully. Can the listeners line up the three players in order of pitch from the lowest-sounding tube to the highest?

Questions you might ask

• Whose tube made the lowest sound? Why? (It is the longest.)

• Whose tube made the highest sound? What do you notice about the length of this tube? (It is the shortest.)

3. Let small groups of children experiment with the tubes to find three different pitches. Each group keeps its tubes for the next activity.

What you will need

• A collection of cardboard or plastic tubes of different lengths but same diameters (eg open-ended foil inner tubes or poster tubes).

• Several tappers (ovals of corrugated card about 15cm long by 10cm wide).

What you will need

- The high-, medium- and low-sounding sets of tubes which the groups identified in the previous activity.

- Printout of the *Tapping tube trio* score to display to the class.

Teaching tip

A conductor may hold a pointer vertically and move it slowly along the score from left to right to help the children know when to play.

When notating their trio, the groups might for example:

– number the tubes and write a number code for the players
– colour the tubes and write a colour-coded chart.

Tapping tube trio

1. Show the class the *Tapping tube trio* score. Ask these questions to help the children understand the score.

Questions you might ask

- How many tubes are playing? (Three.)

- How many pitches are there? (Three.)

- Which tube on the score plays the highest sounds? (The shortest tube; the tubes in the top row.)

- Which tube plays the lowest sounds; in-between sounds? (The longest tubes, bottom row; the middle-sized tubes, middle row.)

- When are the tubes silent? (In the gaps between the symbols.)

2. Divide into the small groups from the previous activity, each with their own set of tubes and a copy of the score. Give the children the score without suggesting an interpretation initially, as they may happily work out their own ideas. If they need direction, suggest these choices:

   – play one sound per symbol;

   – play one repeating rhythmic pattern per symbol;

   – play freely whenever your symbol appears.

3. Ask each group to practise the trio, with or without a conductor, and give them opportunities to perform their interpretations of the score to the others.

4. Now ask the groups to create a new trio and a new way of notating it. Each group passes their trio notation to the neighbouring group for performance. Are the groups happy with the interpretations? Do some notations work better than others? Can they be adjusted to improve them?

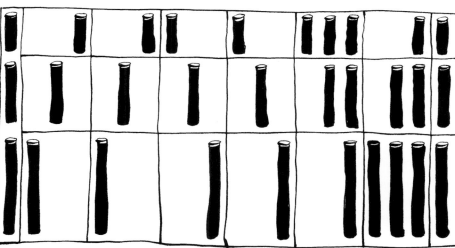

Pitch Stamping tubes

Pitch walls

1. Teach the class this chant, saying the words evenly and rhythmically. Quietly tap the word rhythm with fingers on palms as you say each line:

   Can you play this rhythm?
   I can play this rhythm.
   I can play this rhythm.

2. Divide the class into three groups and repeat the chant like this:

   Group 1 says line 1 in a high voice;

   Group 2 says line 2 in a medium voice;

   Group 3 says line 3 in a low voice.

3. Show the children the printout of this notated on a pitch wall:

Can you play this rhythm?		
	I can play this rhythm.	
		I can play this rhythm.

high voice

medium voice

low voice

4. In the same three groups, the class performs this pitch wall of the chant, in which group 2 chants the first line, groups 1 and 3 the second line, and all chant the final line:

	I can play this rhythm.	**I can play this rhythm.**
Can you play this rhythm?		**I can play this rhythm.**
	I can play this rhythm.	**I can play this rhythm.**

5. Divide into groups of three, each with a set of three different-sized instruments. The groups practise playing the two pitch walls, this time using the instruments to play the rhythm of the chant words.

6. Give the groups printouts of the blank pitch walls and ask them to devise their own patterns using the rhythm of this chant, or one of their own devising. They may like to play their idea first, then notate it on a blank pitch wall; alternatively, they may notate their idea, then play it to see whether they like the results. Ask individual groups to demonstrate their walls.

What you will need

- Three sound-makers of different pitch for each group, eg

  – three plastic tubs: small, medium and large;

  – three drums: small, medium and large;

  – three xylophone bars: short, medium and long;

  – three tapping tubes: short, medium and long.

- Printouts of the pitch walls. WB

Teaching tip

The words of the chant can be any short, rhythmic phrase that you or the children choose.

• • • high low • • getting higher • • getting lower • • staying the same • •

What you will need

 40))) 44

Listen to Stamping tubes

Questions you might ask

• At the very beginning, what is the order of pitch of the first three sounds you hear? (High, low, medium.)

• Do you hear this pattern again? (Yes, it is repeated many times, but with other sounds added.)

• After the music stops briefly in the middle of the piece, what do you notice about the pitch? (It changes – there are some higher sounds.)

Ask the children if they know how the sounds are being made. Did anyone recognise a similarity between the tapping tubes the class made and the sounds in the music? You may like to refer them to the printout illustration of the stamping tube players.

Pitch buildings

What you will need

 WB 14

• Three sound-makers of different pitch for each group as before.

• The groups' pitch walls, devised earlier.

I. Discuss the ways in which the groups might make buildings out of their pitch walls, eg

– play one pitch wall several times;

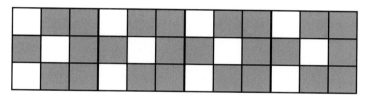

– use more than one pitch wall and decide how many times to play each;

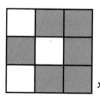 x 3 x 5 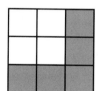 x 2

– join up with another group to play your pitch walls at the same time;

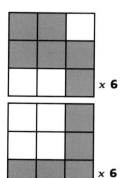 x 6

x 6

– join up with several groups and play your pitch walls one group after another.

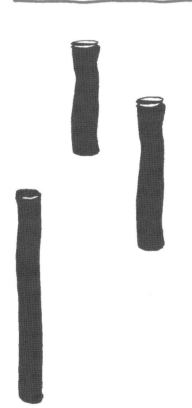

Pitch round up

When the children have completed the pitch activities in this section, give them opportunities to listen out for and comment on pitch in other sections. Here are some examples:

La Volta

Ask the children to notice the accompaniment to each version.

What you will need

🎵 16-17)))

Questions you might ask

- Version 1 (track 16): does the pitch of the accompaniment stay the same, move higher or move lower? (It stays the same.)

- Version 2 (track 17): can you describe the pattern of pitches you hear in the accompaniment. (There are three pitches which jump up from low to medium to high, again and again.)

Winds on the mountain

Listen to the whole piece and compare the pitch of the three sections.

What you will need

🎵 12-14)))   🎵 45

Questions you might ask

- Would you describe the pitch of the panpipes which play the melody at the beginning of the piece as high or low? (Low.)

- Do the next two sections sound the same general pitch or different? (The fast section sounds mainly high, the last is low.)

Listen to the beginning of **Winds on the mountain** before the charango enters. The melody is played on panpipes. It is in four short phrases. Ask the children to draw with their hands in the air the pitch shape of the phrases. (The shapes are given on printout 45.)

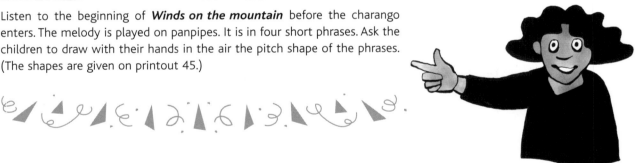

ASSESSMENT GUIDANCE

Can the children:

- ★ make long and short sounds using their voices?
- ★ discriminate between different pitches?
- ★ control their voices to explore a wide range of pitch?
- ★ use their voices to sing melodies with a developing accuracy of pitch?
- ★ perform from notation which represents pitch?
- ★ notate their own melodies using simple pitch notation?
- ★ describe the use of pitch in music?

Structure introduction
· · · ·beginning middle end· · · · ·repetition· · · · ·contrast· · · ·

ABOUT THE STARTER ACTIVITY

Rhythm rondo WB – performing a body percussion pattern (**A**), and improvising contrasting clapping patterns (**B**, **C**, **D** etc) to make a rondo structure: **A B A C A D A E**...

WHAT YOU NEED TO KNOW ABOUT STRUCTURE

★ Music can be structured in a variety of ways.

★ As we listen to a piece of music we become aware of repetitions and patterns, and of combinations of different sounds which together make a coherent whole.

★ Sometimes sections of music are organised in a simple, regular structure, which we can readily recognise as we listen, eg the **A** and **B** sections of binary form (two related but contrasting sections), the **A B A** sections of ternary form (in which the first of two contrasting sections is repeated), or the **A B A C A** sections of rondo form. (Structure and form are interchangeable terms.)

★ In other pieces of music the sounds may not be grouped in these regular arrangements and we may at first be less aware of how they are ordered.

★ In addition, all music is made up of varied combinations of its elements – duration, timbre, texture, dynamics, pitch, tempo – and it may be the way in which these are used which gives a piece its shape and form.

★ Through *Rondeau* and *Kartal*, the children will explore rondo form and how to consider the elements within this structure.

What you will need

 WB 15

• Space for the children to sit in a circle.

Rhythm rondo

1. Teach the children this body percussion pattern:

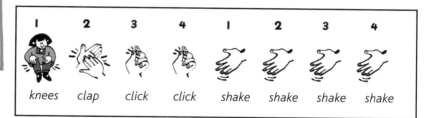

| **1** | **2** | **3** | **4** | **1** | **2** | **3** | **4** |
| knees | clap | click | click | shake | shake | shake | shake |

Keep repeating over and over again, counting out loud at first, then silently in your heads.

Questions you might ask

• How many times do we count to four before repeating the pattern? (Twice.)

• What is different about the first group of four actions and the second? (The second group is silent.)

2. Explain that the first four actions are the **A** section of a rhythm rondo. The children are going to take turns round the circle to make contrasting patterns for **B**, **C**, **D**, **E** etc sections of the rondo. Invite volunteers to demonstrate new body percussion patterns during the four silent shakes, then play the game round the circle:

A	B	A	C	A	D	A
1 knees **2** clap **3** click **4** click	**1** shoulders **2** shake **3** clap **4** clap	**1** knees **2** clap **3** click **4** click	**1** stamp **2** clap **3** stamp **4** click	**1** knees **2** clap **3** click **4** click	**1** click click **2** stamp **3** click click **4** stamp	**1** knees **2** clap **3** click **4** click

Structure Rondeau

WHAT YOU NEED TO KNOW ABOUT RONDEAU

★ Composer: Johann Sebastian Bach (born Eisenach, 1685–1750).

★ Bach's *Rondeau* (the French spelling of rondo) is the second of seven pieces in his *Suite no 2* for orchestra.

★ Bach was one of several composers of his time who composed suites – each one a group of short listening pieces based on dances popular across Europe. His *Rondeau* gives the impression of a stately and elegant court dance.

★ Bach's orchestra for this suite consists of:

– a small number of **strings** – **violins**, **violas**, **cello**, **double bass**;

– solo **flute**;

– **harpsichord**.

★ As you listen to *Rondeau* (track 41) try to pick out the orchestral features listed below to identify the different sections: **A A B A C A**. This will enable you to help the children recognise them:

A – the whole orchestra plays; the melody is played by flute and violins; the cello, double bass and harpsichord play a bass line under the melody;

A – repeat of A;

B – at the beginning, the harpsichord and lower strings drop out; at the end, a melody is played by the cello;

A – repeat of A;

C – the flute starts this section with a running step-by-step melody; at the end, the harpsichord and lower strings stop playing until the return of section A;

A – repeat of A.

ABOUT THE ACTIVITIES

Listen to *Rondeau* – recognising the sections of the rondo.

Rondeau dance: A section – learning simple dance steps for the A section of the rondo.

Rondeau dance: B and C sections – devising steps for the B and C sections.

Listen to *Rondeau* – noticing additional elements which help us to identify the different sections.

Rondeau dance steps – *call the steps as the music plays*

One step left, one step right,
Swing hands up then swing
    them down,
Swing hands up then swing
    them down,
One step left, one step right,
Swing hands up, let go,
    then turn around.

One step left, one step right,
Swing hands up then swing
    them down,
Swing hands up then swing
    them down,
One step left, one step right,
Swing hands up, let go,
    then turn around.

Your own steps

(The children make up their own steps to contrast with the A section; see page 56.)

• • • •beginning middle end • • • • • •repetition • • • • •contrast • • • •

What you will need

Listen to Rondeau

Ask the children to listen to the piece all the way through once.

Questions you might ask

- What did you notice about the first melody you heard in this music? (It kept coming back again.)

- Did you hear any other melodies? (Yes, they were in between.)

- Listen again, asking the children to raise a hand each time they hear the **A** section melody, and lower it during the **B** and **C** sections. It may help if they sing the **A** melody.

What you will need

- A large space or hall.

Teaching tip
The dance steps for the A section are called on track 42.

Rondeau dance - A section

1. Teach the A section dance steps.

   In small groups the children form circles holding hands.

2. Call the steps of the A section as the music plays, and repeat until the children are confident with the movements. They may like to call the steps with you as they perform them, but aim to perform the dance without any calling when it is fully familiar.

One step left, one step right,
Swing hands up then swing
      them down,
Swing hands up then swing
      them down,
One step left, one step right,
Swing hands up, let go,
      then turn around.

Your own steps

(The children make up their own steps to contrast with the A section; see page 56.)

One step left, one step right,
Swing hands up then swing
      them down,
Swing hands up then swing
      them down,
One step left, one step right,
Swing hands up, let go,
      then turn around.

Structure Rondeau

• • • •beginning middle end • • • • • •repetition• • • • • •contrast • • • •

Rondeau dance – B and C sections

What you will need

• A large space or hall.

1. Working in their small groups, the children devise their own steps for sections **B** and **C** to contrast with section **A**. They may like to try some of these ideas:

   – four steps into the centre of the circle and four steps back;

   – in pairs, link arms and walk round in a circle, then change direction and repeat;

   – in pairs hold hands at shoulder level and promenade around the circle.

3. When they are ready, ask the groups to demonstrate their new dance steps. Give time for comment from the other groups and suggestions for improvement.

   When they are satisfied with their dance moves, let each group perform their complete dance, **A A B A C A**, to *Rondeau* (track 41).

4. Finally all the groups perform at the same time. Each group's **B** and **C** sections will differ, but during the **A** section all of the groups will be dancing the same steps, emphasising the structure of the music.

Teaching tip

Note that section B has six phrases of music, section C has eight.

The children will need to be very familiar with the music to make up their own steps and, ideally, should have their own access to the recording.

Listen to Rondeau

What you will need

Ask the children to listen out for any additional elements, which help us identify the different sections, eg

A – the melody is repeated at the beginning of the piece so we quickly recognise it. The texture is thickest in this section.

B – at the beginning the texture is thinner and the timbre changes as the lower strings and harpsichord drop out.

C – the music is mainly quiet. The timbres of the flutes, upper strings and harpsichord are heard together at the beginning, followed by a thinner texture when the harpsichord drops out.

Structure Kartal

• • • •beginning middle end• • • • •repetition• • • • •contrast• • • •

ABOUT THE ACTIVITIES

Listen to *Kartal* – identifying the rondo structure of the piece and noticing the similarity to *Rhythm rondo*.

Concentration rondo – learning a chant and body percussion pattern (**A** section). While the body percussion continues throughout, individual children add words on a chosen subject to make contrasting sections (**B**, **C**, **D**, **E** etc).

Animal elements rondo – constructing a class rondo, in which the contrasting sections feature one set of animals and one musical element each.

WHAT YOU NEED TO KNOW ABOUT KARTAL

★ Kartal is the name of the percussion instrument heard in this piece of music from Rajasthan in Northern India.

★ The instrument consists of a pair of thin hardwood blocks, about 15 x 5 cm.

★ The player holds one pair in each hand and skillfully claps them together to produce complex and rapid rhythms, while twirling arms and hands.

★ The structure of the piece can be described as a very free rondo:

A – a rhythm pattern, based on a unit of four counts, is firmly established at the beginning. It is repeated ten times.

B – a different rhythm pattern interrupts.

A – returns.

C, **D**, **E** etc – several more contrasting patterns follow, always alternating with A. These contrasting patterns become increasingly exciting as the player demonstrates his skill. The original A rhythm does not return at the end of the piece.

Listen to Kartal

Questions you might ask

• Can you describe the structure of this piece?

• How is it similar in structure to our *Rhythm rondo*? (There is a section which keeps returning and in between there are different sections. It is a rondo.)

• Can you hear a long pattern which sounds like galloping horses? (It is just before the ending.)

• Can you clap the final pattern? (It sounds like 'da-didi-dada' repeated.)

What you will need

 45)))

Concentration rondo

1. Remind the children of the **A** section body percussion pattern from *Rhythm rondo*. Repeat the pattern several times without the gaps for the other sections.

2. Now teach this chant, accompanying it with the **A** section body percussion:

What you will need

46)))

A	1	2	3	4
	Con –	cen –	tra –	tion,
	Con – cen –	tra – tion,	use your	mind.
	Keep	in	rhy –	thm,
	Keep in	rhy – thm,	words to	find.

3. When everyone can perform the body percussion and chant confidently, agree on a number of subjects for the contrasting rondo sections, eg insects, transport, flowers, colours. List the subject words where all can see them, and ask the children to suggest a number of words for each, eg insects – bee, moth, beetle, spider, fly...

4. Now play *Concentration rondo*. Sit in a circle and all perform the **A** section. Then as you continue the body percussion, call out a subject. The first person in the circle says a subject word, and as the percussion continues, the children take turns to say a word.

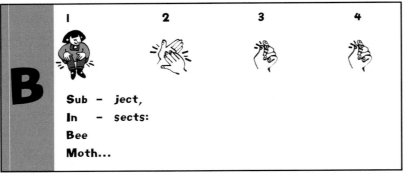

B	I	2	3	4
	Sub - ject,			
	In - sects:			
	Bee			
	Moth...			

As soon as one child falters, count four beats and return to the **A** section and a new subject.

Animal elements rondo

I. Divide the class into:

Ostinato group – this group plays throughout;

A section – *Concentration* melody group;

B C D E F G – six animal elements groups.

2. Teach the ostinato group their part (printout 45. Remind the children of the body percussion pattern from *Rhythm rondo*, then replace the body percussion with the notes C D G G

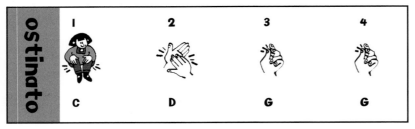

ostinato	I	2	3	4
	C	D	G	G

3. Teach the **A** section – *Concentration melody* (printout 45). Remind the children of the *Concentration rondo* chant, then replace the syllables of the chant with the melody notes (opposite).

4. The ostinato and **A** section groups should practise combining their parts: the ostinato group starts the piece by playing two cycles of their pattern, and continues throughout.

ostinato ostinato ostinato...

A - Concentration

Teaching tip
Let the children play the game on their own in small groups.

You can hear a sample round of the game on track 46.

What you will need

 45-46

• Ostinato group: printout of the ostinato card and low-pitched instruments, notes C D G.

• **A** section group: printout of the **A** section *Concentration* melody card and tuned instruments with notes C D E G A.

• Animal elements groups: printouts of the animal cards and enough untuned or tuned instruments for all to play.

• One bell (eg Indian bells, cow bell or small gong).

• • • •beginning middle end • • • • • •repetition• • • • •contrast • • • •

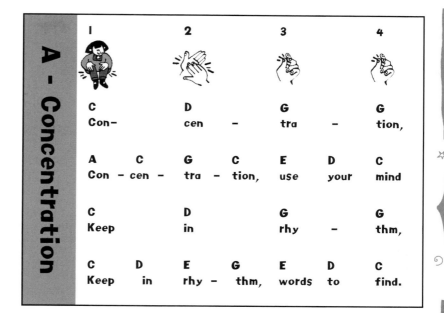

A – Concentration

	1	2	3	4
	C Con–	D cen –	G tra –	G tion,
	A C Con – cen –	G C tra – tion,	E D use your	C mind
	C Keep	D in	G rhy –	G thm,
	C D Keep in	E G rhy – thm,	E D words to	C find.

5. Compose the contrasting sections – **B C D E F G**. Allocate one animal set and one element to each group and give each their corresponding animal card (printout 46):

B **birds** – duration

C **African predators** – dynamics

D **river life** – tempo

E **mini-beasts** – timbre

F **ocean creatures** – texture

E **night life** – pitch

Discuss with each group how to feature their element in a sound depiction of their animal set. The birds group (duration) might consider different bird calls, making contrasts of long and short sounds with their instruments; the river life group might consider the different speed at which their creatures move: flitting dragonflies and fish and slow-moving pike in rushing streams and slow rivers, and so on.

The length of each section may vary, but the end of each must be signalled by striking a gong or bell once.

6. When the groups are ready to perform, place the animal cards in sequence where everyone can see them to remind the players of the order in which the groups play (shown on printout 46). Remind the ostinato group that they will continue to play quietly throughout; the *Concentration* group plays only for the **A** sections of the piece.

Teaching tip

Encourage each animal group to devise ways of notating their music, eg using a sound picture as in *Night music*, or a chart as in *Tapping tube trio*, a *Pitch wall* or a melody grid as in *La Volta*.

Structure round up

When the children have completed the structure activities in this section, give them opportunities to listen out for and comment on structure in other sections. Here are some examples:

Tomorrow the fox, Dis long time, gal

Both these pieces are in binary form, **A B**, familiar to children through the many songs which have two main sections – a verse, **A**, and a chorus, **B**. Ask the children how they can recognise the difference between the verse and the chorus in each piece.

Tomorrow the fox
The verse and chorus lyrics are different: the chorus lyrics stay the same each time; the verse lyrics change in each verse.

The verse and chorus melodies are very similar but the chorus melody is a little longer – it has an extra two phrases in the middle ('And cry as loud as you can call: Woop! woop! woop! woop! woop!')

Dis long time, gal
The verse and chorus lyrics are different: the chorus lyrics stay the same each time; the verse lyrics change in each verse.

The verse and chorus melodies are different.

Winds on the mountain, La Volta, Unsquare dance

All of these pieces are in ternary form, **A B A**. Ask the children to listen to the pieces one at a time and identify the difference between the **A** and **B** sections.

Winds on the mountain
The melody is repeated but the tempo changes:

A slow	**B** fast	**A** slow

La Volta
The A melody is repeated several times, then changes to the B melody, which is also repeated several times, before a return to the A melody. Both melodies are decorated by the solo instrumentalist who improvises little changes to the melody on each repeat.

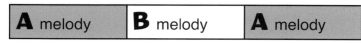

A melody	**B** melody	**A** melody

Unsquare dance
After an ostinato introduction (double bass and clapping) there are three sections in which the instruments change.

A piano	**B** drum	**A** piano

What you will need

(•) 28)))

(•) 38)))

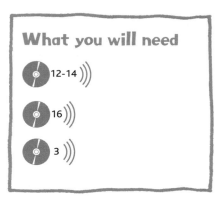

What you will need

(•) 12-14)))

(•) 16)))

(•) 3)))

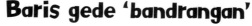

What you will need

(◎) 10))

Baris gede 'bandrangan'

As the children learned in the Tempo section (pages 19-24), a characteristic feature of gamelan music is the vertical layering of long and short sounds. Instruments with the lowest pitch play a repeating melody very slowly with long sustained sounds. Each higher group repeats the melody at double the speed of the previous group. The effect is of many layers of long, in-between and short sounds.

There are also overall tempo changes (the second extract from the music is much faster overall, and there is a big slow down in tempo towards the end). The composer also uses vivid changes in dynamic (lead by the drummer) and texture to create exciting contrasts in the progress of the music.

What you will need

(◎) 8))

Inspector Morse

Questions you might ask

• How has the composer organised the sounds in this piece? (It begins with a repeating electronic morse code rhythm – an ostinato – which continues all the way through the music. The violins take over the same rhythm and play it at different pitches. Other instruments play a long, smooth melody line while the ostinato continues. The electronic signal returns and the music ends quietly as it began.

What you will need

(◎) 29))

Five pieces for orchestra, no I

Webern's intention to create a 'very calm and delicate' miniature for orchestra led him to select a particular series of sounds, each for its own distinctive timbre. The sounds are played individually or are combined together in an airy, open texture. The dynamics are very quiet throughout and the sounds are mostly smooth and long.

Questions you might ask

• What do you like about this piece?

• How is it different from some of the other pieces we have listened to?

• Do you think the composer has been successful in creating 'a very calm and delicate' piece of music?

ASSESSMENT GUIDANCE

Can the children:

★ perform pieces of music in simple structures, including ternary and rondo?

★ understand how the musical elements can be used within simple structures?

★ compose music using simple structures, eg ternary and rondo, with an awareness of the use of the musical elements?

★ describe how the elements are combined and organised in simple structures?

Melody lines

Communication

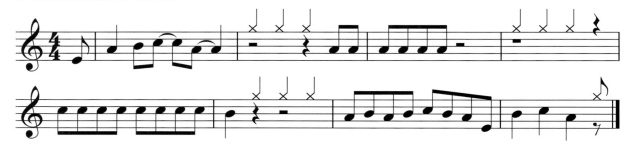

La Volta (simplified)

La Volta

Tomorrow the fox

Dis long time, gal

Didlan (The Ash Grove)

Acknowledgements

The following have kindly granted their permission for the use of copyright recordings included on the accompanying CD:

Art of Landscape for **Winds on the Mountain**, performed by Incantation (Simon Rogers, Mike Taylor, Forbes Henderson) from CD NAGE 101 © 1982 Art of Landscape.

The Decca Record Company Ltd for **Tomorrow the fox will come to town** from `Music from the Time of Elizabeth I', performed by the Academy of Ancient Music/ Christopher Hogwood CD 4331932 P 1982 The Folio Society © 1982 The Decca Record Company Ltd.

EMI Records Ltd for **La Volta** performed by David Munrow and the Early Music Consort of London from `The Instruments of the Middle Ages and Renaissance' HMV SLS 988 P 1976 © 1976 and **La Volta** performed by David Munrow with Christopher Hogwood and Gillian Reid from `David Munrow Introduces and Performs Mediaeval and Renaissance Music' CFP 4384 P 1982 © 1982, by kind permission of EMI Records Ltd and the estate of David Munrow.

Genevieve Dournon for *Claquette-Tap Dances* (**Kartal**) from Rajasthan © 1990. Used with permission.

Hugo Zemp for *Bambous Pilonnants* (**Stamping tubes**) © 1990 Hugo Zemp. Used with permission.

King Record Co Ltd for *Gamelan Gong Kebyar* of `Eka Cita' (**Baris gede 'bandragan'**) Abian Kapas Kaja from © CD KICC–5154. Licensed by King Record Co Ltd, Tokyo, Japan

Sain Recordings Ltd for arrangement of traditional air 'Llwyn Onn' (**Didlan**) by Plethyn (Healy, Griffiths, Gittins) © Cyhoeddiadau Sain 1994, from 'Seidir Ddoe' by Plethyn, Sain SCD 2083 P 1994 Sain (Recordiau) Cyf.

Sony BMG Music Entertainment (UK) Ltd for **Rondeau** from *Orchestral Suite No 2* BWV1067 by Bach, performed by La Petite Bande from CD GD77008 © 1990 Harmonia Mundi Freiburg and for **Orchestral Piece No 1** from *Five Orchestral Pieces Op 10* by Webern performed by the Juilliard String Quartet and the London Symphony Orchestra conducted by Pierre Boulez ©1978 Sony BMG Music Entertainment. Courtesy of Sony BMG Music Entertainment (UK) Ltd. Licensed by Sony BMG Commercial Markets UK.

The Valentine Music Group for **Unsquare Dance** by Dave Brubeck, performed by Dave Brubeck Quartet from CD CRS 32046, © Copyright 1961 by Derry Music Co. USA. All rights for World controlled by The Valentine Music Group, 7 Garrick Street London WC2E 9AR.

All other recordings are copyright A & C Black: **Dis long time, gal** performed by Dog Kennel Hill Primary School Steel Band; **Match up memory** performed by 'Folies Bergères'; **Communication** song performed by Rosamund Chadwick; **Inspector Morse** performed by Missak Takoushian; all other vocals performed by Kevin Graal; remaining tracks devised and performed by Helen MacGregor, Sheena Roberts and Stephen Chadwick.

All rights of the producer and of the owner of the works reproduced reserved. Unauthorised copying, hiring, lending, public performance and broadcasting of this recording prohibited.

Second edition 2007
A&C Black Publishers Ltd
38 Soho Square, London W1D 3HB
© 2007, 1995

ISBN 978-07136-8296-0

Printed in Great Britain by Caligraving Ltd, Thetford, Norfolk

Text © 2007, 1995 Helen MacGregor
Illustrations © 2007, 1995 Alison Dexter
Sound recording © 2007, 1995 A&C Black
Cover illustration © Moira Munro
Interactive whiteboard CD-ROM © 2007 A&C Black

Edited and developed by Sheena Roberts
Designed by Fiona Grant
Sound engineering by Stephen Chadwick
CD-ROM post-production and interactive whiteboard activity authoring by Big Heart Media/Studiotonne

All rights reserved. No part of this publication may be reproduced or used in any form or by any means – photographic, electronic or mechanical, including photocopying, recording, taping or information storge and retrieval systems – without the prior permission in writing of the publishers.

Printouts referred to in the text and contained on the accompanying CD-Rom may be freely printed out and photocopied by the purchasing educational establishment for the educational purposes specified in this pack.

Single User Licence
Please note that the copyright holders have licensed the material in this publication for single use only. The purchaser/licencee is permitted to:

– make one exact and unmodified copy of the Listening to Music Elements Age 7+ CD-Rom (including but not limited to the Intellectual Property Notices) in machine-readable form solely for backup or archival purposes providing this copy is kept in the purchaser's possession.

If you have any queries about the manner in which you may use the material, please contact music@acblack.com

www.acblack.com

SHEFFIELD HALLAM UNIVERSITY
WL
TP 780
MA
ADSETTS LEARNING CENTRE